The Adolescent and His Will

The
Adolescent
and His
Will

::

CALEB GATTEGNO

OUTERBRIDGE & DIENSTFREY
New York
Distributed by E. P. Dutton

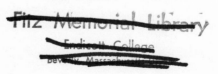

Design: Anne Hallowell

This edition is a revised version of a translation
originally prepared by Mrs. Barbara Weiskrantz.

Outerbridge & Dienstfrey
200 West 72 Street New York 10023

Preface

WHEN the publishers told me of their intention to bring out a revised edition of the English translation of a book I wrote in French more than twenty years ago, I did not think I should agree.

Their reasons were that its content and proposals not only are unknown to most teachers in this country but also are still valid and could be helpful at this moment when adolescence is being discussed by everybody.

Twenty years of reflection, of experimentation, of revision of viewpoints, made this work, as I looked back on it, seem in many ways a milestone rather than a final station. Unable to rewrite it at this time, unable to re-create the inner atmosphere of the time when its content came to me in the form it took in that book, I had a hard time in supplying the few variations required by the editor.

My hope is that this vastly improved translation, with the numerous deletions, clarifications, and added examples will be less difficult to read than the original. If it is, all the merit goes to the editor. My thanks to him expressed here will be the only testimony of a vital contribution to the usefulness of this work.

To the reader I owe a number of explanations which I shall place at the beginning of the book as warning, as well as in order to help dispel misapprehensions.

As I came to the problems examined in the book, problems that interested me because of my temperament and the circumstances of my life, it often occurred that the existing literature was not sufficient to cover what was there to be gleaned. One consequence is that I often use words in ways which are not the current ones. New definitions would perhaps help but I have not always found it necessary. Instead I let meanings emerge from as many situations as are necessary to round up the new notions, as a novelist would do with characters, involving them in scenes that make them more understandable.

My claim generally is that I work as a scientist, that is, that I consider my function one of describing what is by attempting to see the reality behind the appearances. But perhaps my presentation strikes people as more poetry than science. If this is so, such an effect has not been deliberately sought. My temperament, which I should subdue totally to be a good scientist, has been too big a problem for me, and what I could not handle I leave to those who may be enough interested by the subject to pursue it and correct any errors. I always claim that the knower is part of knowledge and that objectivity is an illusion, although like all scientists I attempt to subdue the unique in me in order to find the common in all.

In fact, this is my method of work. Necessarily my investigations begin with me—I must become aware of something before I can entertain it. From this awareness, examined with my inner criteria and compared with observations (necessarily filtered through my self) of others of differing ages, circumstances, times, I reach an expression which I offer as a universal finding. Because I take these precautions of relating my findings to age, culture, viewpoint, I believe I do reach universals and give my work a validity that holds for others than my own curious self.

Sometimes this method makes me a scientist and sometimes an educator. If I stop at the statement of the finding, I am the first; if I take it to the public arena for all to use, I am the latter. So I may belong to a new breed of scientist, the one who does his studies at the pure and applied levels simultaneously.

Since the world is my laboratory and since the world is mainly characterized by its complexity, to succeed in my studies I found it necessary to develop methods as complex as the questions examined. This divergence from the classic Cartesian-Baconian analytic approach so successful since about 1620, I accept as a fact of life. My only specialization has been to learn to accommodate more and more data relevant to *my understanding* into the construct which was to help that understanding. I was conscious that in order to be true to what I was engaged in understanding I could only move towards more complicated, more articulate models using more parts simultaneously, as, say, sight or memory do.

All this does not make my work easy to grasp. Linear exposition is inadequate and the sequence of sentences I use here is totally insufficient to convey all that crowds my mind. Hence, I can only ask readers to go over some passages till by some mysterious process the sequence of words is replaced by illumination.

Perhaps I shall be allowed to say that sometimes I have devoted tens and tens of years in silent examination of some field before I felt I could utter the first word on it in a publication or public statement. For these years of work I ask for some hours of letting the vision seep in.

One more word on this. Unfortunately, communication does not follow from expression. The second is necessary for the first, but communication happens only when the miracle of the meeting of two minds takes place. My efforts are made on expression because this involves me and my experience and sensitivity. The rest is beyond me.

In the history of mathematics, only the last hundred years have been able to take us towards a conscious articulation of what the mathematicians were doing. The most daring—those who have been able to offer their conceptions and to find them acceptable to others—have told us that the most comprehensive notions are the least structured and are the most abstract.

Now, the process of abstraction is in fact the same I used to reach speech in my environment when I was only a few months old. But the term abstraction also describes the succeeding levels of mathematical thought when considered historically. Here it might be simpler and more precise to say that the least structured notions—that is, the most abstract—can produce all others by the interplay of additional structures—a perception which is implicit (and sometimes even explicit) in the modern creative mathematics since 1900.

At the end of a century of introspection we are able to understand that an activity of the mind is best studied by those who entertain this activity all day every day. Mathematics is clear to mathematicians first. For those among them who are fascinated not only with the outcome of that activity but by the activity itself, the process of becoming aware of how mathematicians work also engages them, and if they tell us the special ways that they use their self, we may have found the means of making mathematicians rather than just letting them happen.

In this book I have followed a similar road. I had noticed during my adolescence changes within me that distinguished this time from my childhood. Later in my life, I saw what was still at work within me of the understanding that had emerged during the intense (and intensive) searches that marked my adolescence—mine and all others. How to conceptualize all of this?

When I understood that there was a self that represented myself to myself, I related to "it" or "him" or "me" to understand what happened to me in my actual life, inner and outer. To study life in the concrete, and not only for the purpose of writing novels, made me very demanding and very critical of specialized, narrow studies. I moved from one organization of my observations to another until as much as I could gather would fit in, abandoning an organization because of what would not fit in. Slowly emerged ways of handling the immense material accumulated in one life and accessible to an individual from many lives, and the least structured of all notions, the one that can be structured to produce each of the concrete ones needed for local understanding, came to full light. It has several names according to the context. I call it awareness, self, will, and I shift from one to the other whenever I sense a shade of meaning needed for more precise understanding.

I am struck today by the close analogy of my evolution as a conscious being and the history of mathematics as I see it. Corporately mathematicians have moved from an interest in curious details to the harnessing of the powers which produce all the mathematics conceivable. They found that a small number of notions (some dynamic, some static) would suffice to re-build the "really" interesting mathematics that history has gathered. Similarly, I looked for the powers of "the mind" and found that a small number are sufficient to take us from the objectification achieved by the soma—objectification is one of the new terms I introduce in this book—to the objectifications that constitute the characteristic human works: a symphony, a novel, a cathedral, a political party, a life at peace.

Twenty years ago I could only utter what I was aware of. This book tells the story to that time in the language that I was using then. Since I cannot rewrite it, other works will be needed to bring the story more up to date.

The broad framework of chapters 1-4 is needed to make meaningful the contribution of adolescence to human life. This contribution is spelled out in the final three chapters. Adolescence is nothing for me if not the recasting of experience so that the will can express itself more truly in the rest of one's life. To know the will per se we need to reach ourselves expressing it—consciously or not, freely or not.

One's will is really the hero of this story.

Caleb Gattegno
New York City
January 1971

Table of Contents

1.

Man, A Spiritual Being

IT seems that no one has any difficulty in understanding definitions like these: that man is an animal gifted with language, or an animal endowed with reason or a political animal (Aristotle), or even, for the last century (and even before, as can be seen from the work of Hobbes), that man is a social animal.

These definitions are grasped despite exceptions. Although there are dumb people, it is clear that this does not deny to man the use of language. That man is gifted with reason is not invalidated by the fact that there are fools and savages (one may cure the fools and educate the savages). Although there are solitary or antisocial people, this does not disprove that everyone is dependent on others for survival; the behavior of such people is a proof, if only in a negative sense, of their sociability.

But when man is in question as a spiritual being, no one understands any longer.

The root of this difficulty, I believe, lies in the "small" preconceived idea arising from the constant definition of man as an animal. This preconceived

1

idea is so small that its existence almost always escapes us. Obviously man is an animal. It is so evident that the evolutionary theories have been based on this idea, and we are still looking for the missing link between the "anthropoids" and man (anthropos). It is so evident that most schools of psychology claim the supremacy of the nervous system over consciousness and many believe consciousness to be epiphenomenal. It is so evident that Western societies discovered the illnesses of the body first and then those of the mind (which is also animal) while hardly anybody talks about spiritual illnesses even if we have begun to talk about social traumatisms.

How legitimate is it to consider man as an animal and then, in order to explain his conduct, hunt for that which distinguishes him from his "animalness"? This attitude has not always prevailed. For example, in Genesis, the creation of man is a separate act from that of the animals. The Egyptian, Greek and Roman religions also had different explanations for the presence of man and animals on earth, while the cosmic religions of India place man in the whole of creation (which includes minerals, vegetables, and animals) and at its peak, as does the biological science of the last two centuries.

It is naturally permitted to make any hypothesis one wishes but on condition that it be convincing and that one takes it as a starting point. The hypothesis, for example, that man is an animal. But it is important to remember that it is a hypothesis. Now it is precisely the fate of hypotheses whose apparent obviousness makes them acceptable from the start that they appear as primitive truths to which it would only be necessary to reduce others for these to be explained. It was thus with Newtonian gravitation, for example, which became a source of explanation until the day one asked: what is it really?

Man is an animal. But is he that more than he is vegetable or mineral? And in what sense is he animal?

When the human body is examined, it is seen to be made up of molecules and atoms. It is therefore mineral, even if its components are more particularly of an organic chemical nature. By its molecular structure it is one of the realm of things.

By its cellular structure, it is also vegetable. In fact, by the structure of its tissues it resembles the most developed elements in vegetable life—and by some of its functions as well: sexuality is vegetal.

But the human body becomes animal by reason of its psyche, that is to say because it has behavior patterns. The points of resemblance between man and animal are numerous and one could cover pages enumerating them. The fact that the structures of both are moved to seek food, that actions and perceptions are coordinated for foreseeable ends, will suffice here. Man and animal have so many points in common that it is unnecessary to make this kind of case again in detail.

But let us consider the matter more deeply. It is not by limiting (or overlooking) many aspects of man or by indefinitely extending the "animal idea" that we have arrived at the identification and not simply the partial resemblance of man and animal. When we say "animal" do we not simply mean the whole of the animal kingdom? On the other hand, the man of whom we speak, is it man who is the creator of machines or novels or who manifests certain traditional behaviors, such as hunting, fighting, or looking after his offspring?

These two mistakes seem to be present. On the one hand, our assimilation of man to animal and, on the other, the fact that only a portion of human life is being taken into consideration. The resulting confusion is such that today there exists a science of behavior which calls itself psychology but which only studies that element in man which relates him to the animal kingdom. The same point can be made of the reigning traditional forms of education. They are concerned only with the rational and social animal and never with the whole man.

Let us accept for a moment that behavior is a primitive notion in the sense that it can be reduced to nothing more basic. All animal species can be defined by a behavior which characterizes them alone. The behavior of a donkey may be analyzed, and this behavior would distinguish it from the set of the other animals. It would even be possible to make such a minute analysis that the behavior and instincts of a species could be identified. It is by behavior more than by appearances, which may sometimes differ considerably, that one would define an animal.

In order to link the animal with the vegetable, which is not characterized by a behavior pattern but by a structure or a form, one could say that an animal is a structure fashioned by a behavior pattern. If it were the reverse, the behavior being the result of the structure, it would be difficult to see how a given function came to be, unless it, too (like consciousness), were considered epiphenomenal, which would leave us with the forms, their description and classification by similarities and differences. But then one can still ask: why should we engage in all these behaviors?

A behavior pattern fashioning its own structure:

one could thus properly define an animal species.

But is this an adequate definition of man? Man differs from an animal in that, in order to characterize him, it is usually necessary to group several behavior patterns if not a large number of them.

An animal uses many cells which he organizes in such a way that the instincts of his species may express themselves (this is the behavior). The structure is subordinated to the instinct: an animal becomes an animal by building on this structure, which would be vegetable if it could have survived alone. But it cannot. It dies as soon as the instinct of the species is extinguished by the disappearance of the animal behavior pattern.

Man is capable of several types of behaviors, and it is in so far as he does not consist of a single type that he is a man, that he is healthy.

But one must not understand by this that the behavior patterns succeed each other like a set of photographic slides. In fact they are integrated in an inner life and may be lived separately more or less voluntarily.

If (to restate our definition) each behavior pattern using its own structure is a certain animal, in man there is only one structure to satisfy all behavior patterns. Man is therefore a new synthesis of animal behavior patterns; he is not an animal. Man is herbivorous, frugivorous, and carnivorous with one mouth and the same digestive apparatus; he swims and climbs, hops, walks and floats, lives in all climates, at all altitudes within the same body; for each of these behaviors there exists at least one animal species which has a structure better adapted to it than the structure of man. The latter is several animals united but is in toto not so effective as if he were each one of them. In having all behaviors, he sacrifices quality to quantity—the copresence of many behaviors.

It seems that man, each man, is able to choose the group of behavior patterns which he desires and of which he can make a synthesis (which then will be his personality). A study of his behavior patterns shows this: a man will be artful and cunning, strong and active, vegetarian and industrious, etc.

One could naturally establish for each man, examined from the point of view of behavior patterns, a similar list, and there would be every indication of a scientific analysis in this objective stripping of conducts, an analysis which may be applied to men just as effectively as to animals.

But it would be necessary all the same to consider the synthesis itself.

In fact why should there be such and such a combination of behavioral types? Is it due to chance? Is it necessary to have so many? Is there a principle of selection? Does man arrive in the world already equipped with some behavioral patterns or does he choose them under the influence of social factors? How and why?

So many questions to which it would be necessary to find an answer if one wanted to consider reality such as it appears to us within the framework of behavior patterns!

Again: only to think of the manner in which, at a play and in our reading or when we ourselves are taking some part, we identify ourselves with the imaginary heroes, suffices to understand that there is no theoretical limit to our capacity for adopting this or that behavior. Moreover, necessity often makes one exceed the limits which we think exist. For example, a coward can become a hero in a fire or risk his life to save the lives of his relatives; in a concentration camp a disdainful gourmet fights for the dirty water which takes the place of soup. And this absence of absolute limit in the composition of new behavior patterns, joined to the fact that there is but one structure for them all, means that we cannot define man as a constellation of behaviors, a thing one may validly do for each animal.

It is a peculiarly human faculty to make a synthesis of types of behavior—and many other things as well, as for example, the formulation of a theorem, the creation of a symphony or a new machine, or the foundation of a political party, etc.

Having started with the hypothesis that behaviors were primary notions, we have been led to posit another entity which gives rise to their appearance in the physical structure and which in man also passes beyond the structure and enters into the purely human forms—such is irony, for example—which can only be called spiritual.

Let us take another tack into this question and in order to explain the list of problems suggested above, let us pass from considering behavior to considering the spiritual manifestations of man, of which behavior is a particular case. We shall lose nothing of what the study of behavior would have given us; on the contrary, we are gaining in addition all that the discovery of the spiritual nature of human life can give us.

Human life is spiritual because it is conscious and takes place in space-time: spiritual space-time, perceived only by man. As our study of adolescence will reveal, this spiritual space-time first serves as a framework for action and manifestation, then it is conceptualized, and finally it is directly perceived in the total cosmic and spiritual experience.

It is *not* necessary for us to reproduce all the gestures of a person in order to evoke him, a detail is sufficient—proof that the individual structure, which is a manifestation of the self-structure, is prolonged into space-time and acquires attributes as real as the structure itself.

It is in postponing the study of our spirituality that we heretofore have discovered all other forms of human life. To speak now of the discovery of our spirituality—something always with us, the essential characteristic of man—is one of those strange situations into which we have been forced by the successive absolutes of the past centuries, which regarded us as beings originating elsewhere than in ourselves, created by a power foreign to ourselves, and explaining us from outside. In terms of the absolutes, we were spiritual in so far as the gods or God recognized us as belonging to them, we were rational in so far as we adopted a certain logic, we were free in so far as we subscribed to a certain political, economic or social creed. Outside these absolutes we were: heretics, infidels, deserving of the worst deaths; or prelogicals, or savages or aliens; or slaves, the oppressed, the socially misguided, the exploited.

We only had a right to our spirituality as men when a specific force permitted us to assume it: we had to be a Catholic or live under a democracy, popular or otherwise: to be rich enough, etc. In other conditions, we had to recognize that we had been changed into animals.

But idealism and science have concurred to liberate us from absolutes by revealing to us humanity in its entirety: they have inspired us with the idea of evolution which accustoms us to relativity. In the midst of humanity, we have seen that diverse cosmic conditions carry with them the endless variety of human experiences. With the scientific habit of thinking of natural laws within a given system of reference—temporal in this instance—we have come to understand that behavior patterns were a function of the natural social framework, of man's growth in awareness, and of his power of acting upon the environment.

Cultures, once considered as absolutes in so far as they were behavior patterns, can now be seen as periods in the growth of our awareness that we are evolutionary beings and that this evolution is entirely spiritual. Men are not simply spiritual beings. The spirituality is not just static. Precisely because things change, we can say that men are evolving spiritual energy. Cultures lose their domination when men recognize themselves as such.

All men can recognize themselves as evolving spiritual energy, but all do not want to and the organized environments do not permit or encourage it, either because they themselves have not arrived at this stage of awareness or by a deliberate attempt to restrain it. In fact, it is not easy to forecast what would happen on our planet if all men, simultaneously, became aware that they are an active and creative spiritual energy.

For the moment only a small number of men have succeeded in acquiring the knowledge of themselves as spiritual beings and as evolutionary energy. But as soon as one has acquired this knowledge (the doing of which is simply a movement of one's awareness), it seems very surprising that a particular experience should be necessary in order to attain it. Amongst those who have succeeded, we call educators those who try to lead others to it and men of science those who try to explain the situation as they meet it.

Today, thanks to psychology, man is considered as an evolutionary being in his own life and through successive generations, therefore essentially a temporal being. But the time that is used to measure this temporality is borrowed from clocks, and all the while we are conscious that it is quite insufficient for our real aim, which is to understand and achieve a complete and profound psychological life. From the inventory of the planet, in speaking of the fundamental identity between the inhabitants of the earth, one dares not conclude further than to say: comparative psychology reveals to us a psychological universalism. This thought so far remains an intellectual construct only.

But science offers us on two trays all the necessary elements. It offers us the possibility of not doubting the temporal nature of human life on the physiological plane and it offers us the possibility of discovering in the different social forms, a conscious dynamism which cannot be other than a deliberate human act—which testifies to the presence of this dynamism everywhere on the planet.

The educator, meanwhile, has not the prejudices of the scholar who stops at the point where he believes his tools, tested by a life of cautious successes, can take him no further. The life of the educator is of the future. He lives tomorrow before it arrives. He is a man of action. He does not wait for the scholar to tell him what to believe or do. He outruns the scholar and forms a new generation in his own life, which will only be effective tomorrow. He takes from the trays which science offers him the elements which it keeps separate and sees them united. He makes no *new* synthesis; rather he sees the *reality* which science divides in order to analyze it better. He refuses to make this division because he has chosen to be an educator and not a man of science, because for him science will, in a generation's time, reach the point of saying in precise terms what he seized in a moment and which he transmits in his role as a poet, an inspirer.

If the bulk of science today refuses to consider the spiritual nature of man, who can say that in twenty or thirty years time it will still refuse? The history of science makes one cautious, and too many examples should remind us that it was not always the conservatives, the traditionalists, who were the upholders of truth. The educator, when he is also a scientific man, but a man having recognized for himself his own spirituality, will not be discouraged by the traditional battles between the future which *reaches out* with its truth and the past which holds us back in the shape of organized bodies. He will make it known, loud and clear, that his experience assures him that he speaks of a tangible reality and that everyone can equally well assure himself of it. If people refuse to follow him, then *his* truth, which is *the* truth, will remain outside the awareness of those who refuse him credit and do not try in their turn to reach his level. Still, all his actions will be based on the direct perception of this truth, and if he thus discovers unknown phenomena he may be sure that his pupils will undertake to make them recognized.

The future belongs to the educator who has seized the reality of the spiritual nature of man, because the life of his pupils will be enacted in this future and it is in their interest to find guides for it. The contradiction which society attests to in demanding educators for its children and in refusing to believe them is resolved in the struggle between generations. Today, such a struggle is no longer a necessity. It is another sign of the extension that has been brought about in our understanding of human evolution and its laws, that we can make the struggle of generations disappear by a reconsideration of the duties of the various generations.

Today the true educator no longer doubts the spiritual nature of man. And this knowledge is not just felt, for all his understanding of what it means is expressed in his actions and in the human education which he proposes.

When we have attained the certainty of man's spirituality, we still cannot talk of it properly unless we discover at the same time the singularity of spiritual experience. This experience is accessible to all but can only be attained individually. It is this point that we cannot understand unless love and science guide us. Love, which makes us desire this experience as beneficial for everyone; science, which marvels that only a few achieve it.

If love and science are united in one who attains this evidence of being, an educator is born. An educator who will know how to inspire people, to make them grow by the means which science and love will lead him to discover. These means are sure because they cannot lie to men who have recognized themselves as spiritual energy, and they are effective because they are technically adequate.

Today, few scholars talk of the spirituality of human consciousness, although many discover some aspects of it every day. At the present time, this idea remains, it seems to me, the sole prerogative of educators. So when we offer in this book to prove the spiritual nature of man, we know that we expect an act of faith that perhaps our readers will not want or will not be able to give.

We are not done with this question. For the present it seems sufficient to say that to understand man, who freely unites several behavior patterns in the same structure, we must grasp his spirituality. For to understand what the adolescent experiences, we must first comprehend that man is a spiritual being.

2.   The Psychology
of Affectivity

THE spiritual energy of man manifests itself in many forms. With regard to adolescence, we are concerned specifically with its manifestation in the form of emotions and their expression, for which affectivity will be the technical term.

For those who have studied psychology or the psychologies, the disproportion between the studies devoted to perception, to intelligence, on the one hand, and to affectivity, on the other, is most striking. It is true that psychoanalysis is mainly concerned with affectivity, but does it not obscure the problems in starting from pathology?

I believe that affectivity has been relatively neglected because fundamental prejudices prevented its study and because it is not possible to study affectivity with the methods which have succeeded in the analysis of perception or thought. I also believe that in the domain of psychology, the psychology of affectivity is the field of the future.

But first, what has been seen in affectivity?

Let us begin by examining critically the classical

position which, in my opinion, passed judgment on this domain without understanding it.

Starting with the hypothesis of the duality between the external world and the human being (the duality of mind-body), classical psychology claims that the latter adapts itself to the former and that "all that is found in our intelligence comes from the senses." Perception therefore plays the fundamental role of "adapter"; it is through perception that all conceptions of our relation with the natural and social worlds will be formed.

But if the sense organs relate the human being to the external world, they must relate something which is in the human being to the world. Psychophysiology studies how the brain, and through it consciousness, receives and stores the sense data, and these studies lend weight to a chemical or electrical or physico-chemical theory of the perceptual mechanism. As the sense organs are only a part of the relating system (of individuals to the world) and as the relating activity is pursued beyond sensation—a perception continues after receiving and acknowledging the immediate sensation—it must be admitted that an internal physico-chemical adaptation of the organism exists which prolongs the sensation and allows it to retain its own character. This happens above all in the cases where the preservation of the species depends on it, as for example in the perception of danger.

This adaptation of the internal environment to perception has been called emotion, and emotions are classified according to the somatic characteristics that can be distinguished: blushing, paleness, trembling, fainting, etc., or their various combinations. Emotion is the internal echo of an external or internal sensation, which prolongs the sensation and permits the individual to take adequate action (if this is already organized): for example to flee, or to push, or to jump, etc. So, if we begin with the dichotomy between the world and the senses, we must at least add the emotions to explain the adaptation of the individual to the world.

The classical psychology of affectivity has been the description of emotions and their various associations into sentiments: fear, anger, hatred, love, joy, etc.

Looking at psychoanalysis, we can say that affectivity is the domain where a psychic, biological energy, the libido, develops; this affectivity constructs itself when sentiments follow the laws of psychic development which, when violated, lead individuals or groups to neurosis. These laws, adherence to which brings about the healthy configurations of the libido, are apparent to observers of babies and men alike and are relatively well known. Pleasure and pain guide the sexual instinct in forming the loves and hatreds of babies and children, but social pressure forces these loves and hatreds into either sublimation (through mechanisms equally well known) or repression and neurotic disadaptation. Affective life is therefore essentially one of conflict between the self and the environment: a self, egoist and hedonist par excellence versus an impersonal and exacting environment, whose ends remain transcendental or simply hidden during most of an individual's life. From this view of self and environment comes the importance of the idea of conflict in most of the studies in psychoanalysis and the method which consists in resolving conflicts by leading the subject to become clearly aware of them.

There is obviously an incalculable number of nuances in the detailed analysis provided by psychoanalysts, none of which I have noted here, and because an important number of "successes" in their treatments are recorded, we are assured that their psychology of affectivity has an element of truth in it. We would note, however, that psychoanalysis does not consider affectivity in its general aspect. Affectivity does not represent for atomistic psychology the emotional life as internal responses to perceptions but rather a closed system involving the vicissitudes of a psychic energy. We would further note that the psychic life of sick people—and by *deduction* of healthy ones as well—results from the shock between an energy in the process of being discovered and expressed and a structure which is presented as an absolute, which absolute the psychoanalysts take to be the social and moral structures that direct everyone's living in the group.

Returning to the pair perception-emotion for a moment: one must recognize that the objects of the external world which, according to the physico-chemical laws, ought to affect sense organs that have a similar anatomical structure in the same manner, in fact affect one individual differently from another, and do so all the more when the reactions involve people and animals. Thus the sight of a mouse evokes a different reaction in a woman and in a cat; the first may scream and be terrified, the other licks his lips. A meadow has no effect on a famished lion, but fills a herd of cows with joy. Sensation therefore does not create an emotion except within a particular framework which characterizes the species in the case of animals and the individual in the case of man. It is therefore necessary to have recourse to this frame of reference in order to understand how perception emerges from the external object and how emotion emerges from that perception.

This constitutes a fundamental step forward in the study of affectivity as defined in its classical sense. If one affirms that a perception may create an emotion, the reality perceived must also be defined, and apparently it can only be perceived for animals by means of a species instinct and for man of an individual self. There is no absolute reality for all animals taken together because animals only extract from the collection of all possible perceptions those which their species' instinct allows them to. For the donkey reality includes factors which the tiger cannot perceive, and conversely. The affective lives of the donkey and the tiger, in the classical sense of the term, are only accessible and comprehensible to us when we know how the instinct of their species extracts from the collection of perceptible sensations those to which each can react.

Is it otherwise for us men?

Our expression *external world,* about which philosophers of all ages have passed sleepless nights, should be defined by the psychologists who study the whole of human reality as evolving and as containing life. Other than in these terms, it must be said straightaway that it is an empty expression. There is no external world as such, there is a complex and evolving human reality which is perceived selectively by each individual and by successive generations, perception itself being a deliberate action of the individual self using his sense organs to organize his images (the organization of which will be made meaningful because it agrees with one's actions).

What is clear concerning animals with very different behaviors becomes, in the case of humans, a hypothesis. Yet it is a hypothesis that child psychology and the psychology of abnormal and disturbed people, and also anthropology seem to support. Here, the essential difficulty is that we do not readily recognize that each one of us perceives the totality of the universe differently. We are accustomed by language to the utilization of concepts which replace full reality and standardize it. The result is that we no longer ask the same sort of question with regard to ourselves which makes the difference between animal instincts obvious. We are not preoccupied with knowing if the word chair evokes in one the image of a red, padded chair, and in the other that of a white, wooden chair. We have surmounted our differences in creating a neutral, conceptual language.

But this does not prevent us from no longer understanding each other as soon as we enter a field where language is no longer the standardizing tool. For example, when we speak only one language and do not understand that of our interlocutors, we are thrown back onto our personal perceptions, and we can have contact with strangers only by re-establishing a code based on authentic sensations and emotions which it is up to us to make them share in a way similar to our own.

The field of affectivity—the field of our emotions— differs according to cultures in so far as a culture furnishes a code for translating perceptions into emotions. This can be seen for example in the different reactions which certain foods evoke in a foreigner and a native: perception will engender certain emotions in one by reason of his habits, while the other will have to detach himself from his own culture if he wishes to experience the emotion of the first. In this case, insofar as man adheres to the habits that culture imposes, culture is for man the equivalent of the species' instinct. But the control exercised by culture is only superficial, although it functions for hundreds of millions of people, as does the species' instinct. Those who have freed themselves from culture and who form new habits for themselves prove to us the superficiality of its hold.

Having arrived at this point, we can see that, for animals, the species' instinct is necessary to the constitution of their affectivity (emotional life), while man must disengage himself from established frameworks in order to attain his true emotive life. To the extent that he favors culture, he loses some of his human quality, for he abandons his capacity to process stimuli from outside himself. In adhering to cultural forms which are only transitorily necessary, he creates for himself habits which resemble species' instincts.

The question to which we now turn will bring us closer to our subject. We shall examine affectivity within the framework of what, in the first chapter, we called the spirituality of man and justify, up to the point we have now reached, the belief that the hypothesis that man is a spiritual being is nearer the truth and more useful than the notion that man is an animal.

What follows, I should add, will for some require close reading.

To say that man is an evolving spiritual energy means two things. On the one hand, it means that from the moment one considers that a being is human, one admits that his spirituality is entirely present. On the other hand, it means that this energy is constantly capable of evolution, of going beyond itself, insofar as it is energy. Put another way, this means acknowledging man's evolutionary power just as physicists in the second law of thermodynamics, recognize cosmic energy's power of involution.

These two aspects of the question are very different but are complementary. We intend here to do no more than sketch their significance, for the argument in full is too long to develop.

A human being says he is a spiritual being as he becomes aware of his spirituality. In the same way as we are made aware of our body and of the care to give it, of our intelligence and of the necessity of cultivating it, of our bond with others and of the service that we owe them, we only reach our profound self—another word for which is will—thanks to a special act of finding oneself. This act is frequent in adolescence, and we encounter it in history or in adulthood under the name of *mystical experience.*

Notice that when we reach this recognition of ourselves as spiritual beings, we find ourselves no different from what we were, we simply recognize that our spirituality had been turned elsewhere and was not conscious as it has now become. We recognize that we have always been spiritual beings and look for evidence of our spirituality in the things that occupied us before. This return to our point of departure is very difficult—to begin with, an intellectual hypothesis. We test its reality first on others and then on ourselves as we come to see that we can explain the fact of human life from its beginnings, from the moment that it is manifested in a body and in the life of the baby and the child. We proceed this way—dealing with our recognition as a hypothesis—because we have only a late awareness of our spirituality. No doubt awareness of our spirituality will become possible much sooner when education for spirituality replaces the present education, which, at best, is limited to making a child aware of its intellect and its social functions. The awareness then will no longer be a question of hypothesis but a basic fact which will be asserted in the same way that we today say "man is undeniably a social being . . . . "

In order to make this analysis of the meaning of spirituality clearer, let us accept that the human being is a spiritual energy capable of what we shall call—and here I reintroduce from the preface a term essential for our discussion—objectification. That is to say capable of partially organizing itself and of maintaining in itself this organized fraction. This proposition will certainly not startle a modern physicist, even if it scandalizes the laboratory psychologists. Is not matter in effect objectified energy which coexists in equilibrium with matter?

To objectify itself is a spontaneous function for spiritual energy. But since objectified energy, despite the fact that it is organized, is still energy, it is still available insofar as it can be disengaged and reorganized—as in the case with a hypothesis which is made and then afterwards rejected or with a dream which disappears. I state that spiritual energy is objectified first of all in the human body which is human and spiritual from the beginning, although embryologic physiology and anatomy may refer to it in terms of pure structure. We are present in our initial cell, I am saying, as we are present at the height of our evolution at a certain moment of our adult life. Only we have not yet objectified that which will permit us to become aware of our human spirituality. Also we are still preparing the first human structures, which are somatic and which will remain human all through our life. Physiology in vain seeks for the source of our spirituality or even of our intelligence in the somatic functions. We shall not find the answer in that direction.

The objectification of the body, which takes months, is only one step that spiritual energy will envisage in order to make possible a spiritual human life. To know why is not the issue. It is true that the objectification does not strike one as taking place until, as in Descartes's *cogito,* it is grasped as a thought. Still, it could have been found in all sensory experience and in participation in games, both of which provide other steps of the objectification of spiritual energy as it makes use of the soma already objectified.

The point that the body is an objectification of spiritual energy, so difficult to accept, is, however, partially recognized by all religious faiths and by science, which finds for example in genetic studies the reasons for the impossibility of the fusion of the species. Man, biology shows, is human from the beginning, and this means that the egg in its development is potentially capable of all that man can do. At what moment will this capacity penetrate the somatic structure? Nobody has the answer to this question. Writers like J. E. Marcault (in Marcault and Th. Brosse *L'Education de demain,* Alcan, Paris, 1939) propose an ascent of the energetic spiritual self—of which Marcault made a study—on a pre-existing structure, a view that thereby separates the transmission of the structure (in the domain of physico-chemical heredity) and the self getting hold of it, but such writers do not indicate at what moment this possession becomes possible.

It seems to me much easier to suppose that it is the

function of spiritual energy to build the embryo with all the profound involvement of the physiological mechanisms. Certainly, this spiritual energy is capable of taking the form of that energy which will make the cells out of the molecules provided by the maternal blood. The energy will build the body according to its own laws—some of them studied by embryologists— so that this body will serve the future spiritual functions of a particular man. How could it be otherwise?

To construct an edifice which must perform the human functions, foreseeable or not, supposes the most intimate relation of the spiritual self—which most people admit is present in the adult—with its structure. Is there a greater intimacy than to suppose that the body is an expression of the spiritual self, that objectified part which will permit the self to be according to itself?

The physico-chemical complexity of development, the particular form of generation of the human embryo and its birth are not less mysterious if one does not make this hypothesis, and I would only hope that critics of the view that I advance here will examine their own hypotheses as severely as they will judge mine.

Let us now pinpoint the connection between spirituality and affectivity. Since the spiritual self is, in its manner, present in all its objectifications and the body is spiritual energy objectified, affectivity is the presence of this energy in all the functions of the body.

Affectivity is spiritual energy which knows itself to be present, the means of knowing varying with the times or ages. Emotions are known precisely because of affectivity—they could not function without it—

and they indicate the presence of a part within the totality of spiritual energy. An emotion is known to be human because it is spiritual energy which has been objectified in the physiological and vegetative mechanisms of an individual; affectivity is the maintenance of contact with spiritual energy in the objectifications (which means that the self knows that the body is part of the self and belongs to it and that the body will do what it is ordered to do). Indeed, I would maintain that affectivity is the subtle link with the whole of the cosmos because it is that which is in contact from the beginning with molecules (the mineral world), with cells and tissues (the vegetable world), and with behaviors (the animal world). The human machine only functions as a very complex organism, conceived and maintained and organized by the self, present everywhere in the form of affectivity. Emotions are the dynamic links which maintain contacts between the parts and are themselves part of this entity of affectivity which, although present in each of the parts, is recognized above all in the totality of these parts.

Affectivity and emotions precede perceptions of the outer world; the former are only connected with the latter because images are organized energy: internal reality is constructed prior to that which becomes, following the creation of signs and conventions, external reality. Like affectivity and emotions, the sense organs are also functionally organized by energy (which then is structured by them in turn), and perception is a tool of the self by which it objectifies itself. More specifically, the self may choose its ties with the sense organs, accentuate or loosen them, perceive or obstruct their function. The sense organs are *extensions of the self*—the reversal of the usual perspective. The organ does not perceive what it wants. It perceives "reality" only in so far as it is activated and "educated" by the interior reservoir of images which functionally unite all the senses through the dynamics of energy, or affectivity. In this way we can understand the reason for the perfect adequacy of images to *our* reality, to *our* perceptions, to *our* emotions, and the singularity of this connection for each man in each civilization.

Our perceptions are what *we* do with "sense messages"—therefore what our affectivity does with them, since affectivity is prior to perception (and intelligence results from a certain *one* organization of our perceptions). There is perception or perceptions according to what spiritual energy has done with our organs and our affectivity. The "beauty" of the mountains has not always been seen with our senses, nor was perspective. We have actually reorganized our senses in order to perceive perspective and the mountain's beauty, and it is likewise with everything.

But what must be stressed above everything is that affectivity has always existed in us, that it is so primitive that it is difficult to reach it, as old memories are difficult to recall. If we are traumatized by life, our affectivity does not succeed in setting itself up as it desires, and it is possible that in these cases it is manifested in negative forms, as psychoanalysts claim always would occur. Affectivity not only permits the measurement of *maladjustment* between the spiritual self and the environment—the extent to which the self diverges from the environment; it is on the contrary the source and total measure of *adjustment* of the environment, and it is a matter of astonishment that man should be so adapted to all cosmic conditions of the planet (which no undomesticated animal has been able to do), to all kinds of life, in all civilizations. This proves that he plays a creative role in the environment and that the environment really only exists for him in so far as it is apprehended and integrated by the self.

Since affectivity is constantly present in us and has been from the beginning, how is it that it is not spontaneously manifested as such to the one who seeks it?

It must be said that *it is* manifested but that our preoccupations have led us to deny it its true place, although everyone suspects that this place was very great.

Affectivity is background, it is fundamental life, and it serves action primarily. For a number of years in the beginning of our life, our knowledge of ourselves is reduced to what we feel. For us then, only the world which is accessible to us *is* the world. We live action.* Human action is spiritual, and it spiritualizes the universe that we objectify. Human action does not aim at expressing the simple instinct of preservation as is often stated. Rather it leads us to the knowledge—in our senses, in our perceptions and systems of action, in our emotions—of the "external" universe, which universe we create by living it. Through action our affectivity "animates" the universe of our perceptions, already partly objectified and animated, owing to the fact that perceptions become images. Action enriches images, makes them dynamic in other dimensions, and the universe, which results from it, is thereby spiritualized in the sense that no single element in this objectification of action is necessary. It is pure creation, and differs only

---

*Action is the second of the forms which spiritual energy objectifies, after the body, which makes it possible.

according to the cosmic conditions in which we are born.

The enthusiasm which the child has for action, his will to work out the exact amount of energy needed for each perception and each action are proof that affectivity is present as a basis for his behavior—as a motivating force—and is present in the detail of perceptions and actions.

In the Western civilization man passes a good dozen years at this double dialogue, between the self and its spiritual universe, out of which comes the "world." It is then that the self, having objectified all the elements it needs for action, finds itself in the presence of the creative self, of affectivity per se, and, in spite of the lack of habit in recognizing it, vaguely feels that affectivity is really the self. *This contact with spiritual energy is adolescence.* It is a contact of the self with itself, it is the spirituality of man discovering itself in a new way. Objectification is being slowed down but not life. But it is a contact made possible by means of the objectification that has already occurred. As we shall see later, this contact often leads to conflict instead of leading to the pursuit of the creative function, which was the function of the self up to now.

The loss of this contact is frequent in all civilizations, and there results from it the specialization of human conduct which, while remaining affective, does not recognize that it is so. It seems, however, that this may not be the general fate: the exceptions are the hopeful signs that it can be otherwise.

Today, affectivity, whose presence psychoanalysts and the traumatism caused by being involved in wars has abruptly revealed to us in the West, forces us to make conscious efforts so as to capture the value of human life and to educate men to the desired understanding by friendship and love—in essence, to nurture with this aim the affectivity with which we are in closest contact during adolescence.

The following chapter will be devoted to this question. But to close this one, we shall summarize in new terms the conclusions which emerge from our discussion.

If man is a spiritual being, he must be so in all respects, and we have seen that if the species' instinct in animals creates a form for itself to produce the behavior which this instinct also brings into being, in man the possession of the structure occurs at the same time as its constitution takes place. Affectivity is the presence of spiritual energy in the body, in perceptions, and in actions—a presence which is experienced as the identification of our bodies, our images, our gestures with what is ourselves and which vibrates, thinks and loves.

Affectivity is spirituality which, by means of objectifications, is recognized as distinct and identical at the same time: distinct because mingled with the structure which is organized energy, identical because of its human and spiritual nature. The continuity of our life is not assured by memory, since we forget so many things, but by the current of affectivity, the continuity of spiritual energy objectified or not. Stream of consciousness is only the name given much later to an intellectualized affectivity which is not only felt but also thought. Before this intellectualized affectivity there was the affectivity itself. Affectivity cannot be considered as the collection of emotions unless one limits the first or adds to the latter that which unites them. Emotions are fractions of energy enclosed in the objectifications. They render objectifications spiritual, maintaining them dynamically in the self—which explains the individual coloration of objectifications which may still be socially comparable. The excess or lack of energy in them brings a disequilibrium to their function which can be sufficient to explain a number of traumatisms and some kinds of defective conduct.

It also follows, from this manner of putting the issue, that man's spiritual life includes his somatic life and the life of his actions, and that the successive spiritual dialogues which constitute the act of living demand particular conditions which we shall only be able to reproduce for all men when we understand them. In particular, freedom, of which educators speak as the only favorable climate for the full flowering of personality, may be understood in terms of such a condition—that is to say, a condition permitting the most intimate contact of an active being with its spiritual self, or as a contact between a self and its objectifications. Freedom excludes all social pressures resulting from prejudices, and these are numerous.

We shall see later how affectivity can be educated in order to produce intelligence and love and how the dialogues with the universe which follow adolescence may be sources of new forms and corroborate our definition of man as evolutionary spiritual energy. Affectivity is that form of spiritual energy which is accessible to us today, and it is from it that our psychological reflections will emerge for the time being, in the same way that, in the natural sciences, radioactive emissions, found first, have been used as a guide to cosmic energy itself, postulated yesterday, tangible today.

Affectivity, I am persuaded, is only a "lower" form

of spiritual energy, the one we recognize in the objectifications of our lives. But it is also the sure indication that the reservoir exists and that one must try to reach it. Education of affectivity—this action exerted on it—could lead to the true source which is in us and can make known some manifestations of it which have escaped us because we only see ourselves as externally motivated by moderate forces, even when we imagine colossal spiritual forces in Good and Evil. In the same way, the physicists of the seventeenth century recognized only small forces alongside gravitation.

Aside from establishing certain guidelines for the discussion on adolescence to follow, my wish in this analysis has been to contribute to wider knowledge of a neglected reality, affectivity, and to submit it to the attention of all those who are able to study it. A psychology of affectivity must be elaborated, and the title that I have given this chapter is essentially an invitation to undertake this task.

3.

Education for Love

THE aims and the necessity for this education—and its importance for the subject of adolescence—will clearly emerge when we know what to understand by love.

Now, this term is used in at least three ways which, psychologically, are very different. We shall call them respectively attachment-love, friendship, and universal love, and we shall distinguish them from each other by quickly outlining their salient features.

Attachment-love is essentially egocentric and unconscious; friendship is given to a chosen person who is loved for himself and consciously; in universal love the generalization of the gift of self and of friendship is a positive act by the one who loves and, indeed, everyone who is met by it is embraced by this love to the same degree as all those who have preceded him and all those to follow.

In order to analyze love more completely, we must consider in detail these three levels and understand how they make their appearance and how one passes from one to the other.

*   *   *

It is curious that we should call love the attachment of parents for their children and also the attachment of children for their parents. In fact, at least in the early years, these sentiments are completely different. While a child receives from its parents all the marks of affection that they wish to give him, the very young child does not know what it means to express a sentiment—up to the time when he can use the same manifestations as his parents. While the parents offer the full wealth of their tenderness voluntarily or unconsciously, the child has no other choice but to receive. He forms the habit of receiving because he has no other alternative and from this habit result both the unconsciousness of his behavior and his egocentricity, which are characteristics of his relationship with his parents. His entire behavior results from his certainty that this right is given. In fact, for a number of years, he has all the rights and no duties. He manifests his right to parental servitude by crying and screaming and becomes accustomed to seeing adults regulate their conduct according to his needs. His egocentricity is natural, and his unconsciousness results from the fact that he formed the view of the relationship between his parents and himself from the very beginning of his life. His comprehension of right relationships between himself and an enlarged environment develops much later. Naturally, parents feel themselves rewarded by the smiles of the baby and the opportunity they have to give themselves. (Nonetheless there is a risk of this relationship leading to a deadlock, particularly in the case of an only child who has not learned to develop his affectivity in an alternative way.)

Let us consider more fully a child who naturally

receives from his parents all that they want to give him without their asking anything in return but the acceptance of their love. This is the case of all children for some months at least, often for some years (at times, for some, for the entire life). How does life appear to children in this commonplace relationship? For them, the question of whether to be the center of their parents' interest or not, to accept or not to accept what is spontaneously given without their being consulted, does not arise. Life, such as it appears to each of us, imposes this situation. And the children grow up having fixed in their experience this relationship of receiver of love (themselves) and giver of an acceptable form of relating judged satisfactory by the adult.

At first the adults can only demand of the baby certain gestures, certain contacts, etc. But for the child, the gestures, contacts, etc., become the expression of what is expected of him in return for what he receives, and he rapidly excels in these manifestations. The demand by the adult then gives birth in the child to standard expressions of love. On the basis of his collection of gestures and attentions, which are soon ritualized, he will organize his relations with those who attend to him. He will know that to hug is an affectionate gesture, and similarly with kissing, smiling, etc. But what is the nature of the sentiment with which he invests these gestures?

Being the center of parental tenderness and not using other expressions than those that imitation leads him to adopt, he expresses, in forms which appear clear to the adult, a sentiment which he does not yet feel fully, or at least which is not comparable to what the adult feels. Parents know that they "love" the child and express this to him in a seemingly adequate way. But by the same gestures the child expresses something which he does not fully know yet, and gradually he takes the sentiments with which he endows these forms to be love. It is by this name that the adult labels that experience which the baby is not yet able to feel fully.

The disproportion between the greater or lesser mastery that the parents have of their sentiments and the position of the child with regard to his, leads to an experience of love which is so confused that today we are hardly able to understand it. How many parents are unhappy about the development of their children's sentiments! How many children must undergo very painful conflicts because their entire sentimental life is out of focus due to the discrepancy between the love of their parents for them and the spontaneous love which they themselves experience outside the family!

I believe that an explanation of this maladjustment is found in the two different forms of affectivity that we have just examined—that members of two generations nonetheless speak of the same way. The parents give, the child receives. As the baby is very vulnerable, the parents feel themselves obliged to sacrifice themselves for him, to protect him and to make him the conscious center of their attentions. He becomes accustomed to this situation, the only one he knows, and, conscious of his rights, makes demands. Love appears to him as a necessary link incorporating the whole of life, where the demands made upon others are legitimate and in general satisfied. Attachment-love is the result.

It is this form of love that the child will know and that he will think normal. Having need of all that is required to live and objectify healthily, he finds in his environment, as a pre-existing element, this behavior of his parents and does not doubt that it is his right to be the center of interest of others at the price of the small compensations which his parents demand. He expects from all those whom he meets the attachment shown to him by his parents. He will see in the people constituting his environment friends or foes, according to whether his rights, such as he knows them to be, continue to determine their conduct in his contacts with them.

If he loves someone, it will be in this egocentric fashion, which is why most small children quarrel so easily and immediately separate from their companions when their right has not been spontaneously observed.

The egocentricism of attachment-love does not always disappear with age. How many adults drag it after them and make themselves miserable on its account! It is attachment-love which forms the core of certain very exclusive kinds of maternal love which demand from the child an unlimited devotion to it and to what it stands for. The egocentricism which is natural in one who receives becomes a monstrosity in one who believes he is giving. It is this egocentricism of attachment-love which reduces love to nothing, whether that of mothers and fathers, or of friends and lovers. As it is most often unconscious, it is equally the source of intellectual misery and leads the one who "loves" to establish indefinitely a bookkeeping account of what he has done and sacrificed for the loved one. Is this attachment-love, the most common form of love, love at all?

It leads to all kinds of frustrations and contradictions, precisely because love presupposes a gift, because we can only give what belongs to us, and because attachment-love is unconscious of everything within it, while exclusively expressing itself in terms of rights and demands.

Now imagine a world of adults who are victims of attachment-love and who have not learned to get out of it by themselves, and place them in the world as parents. The results could be hell. Children, inevitably egocentric and unconscious, will receive as a right the wealth of tenderness which, however, is given them by those who can only associate a gift with an account, for whom all gifts must one day be returned. Maternal love, like any other love, may be an investment.

Such a world exists and all the literature on delinquency abundantly confirms it.

I believe that it is in good part because no education for love is given, nor even envisaged, that many people remain bound by the attachment-love which poisons so many lives.

We must return to our hypothesis of the spirituality of man, even poorly understood, to glean a glimmering of hope.

All the while that the child uses other people for his own ends—which are for years the mastery of action—his relations with his companions are those of playmates. But he reaches a point when he has mastered action, and he then enters into simultaneous contact with his own self and that of another. This other is the chosen one. Each of us has known the experience of discovering a friend in his life, the person to whom we choose to bear witness (to use the concepts developed here) to our contact with spirituality through all the experiences of our whole being. These two phenomena—of chosen friend and the recognition of spirituality—are concomitant. They are not independent. They are one and the same experience. We recognize our spirituality in so far as we recognize an *alter ego*, "the other one."

This relationship, that of friendship, is therefore characterized by two traits opposed to attachment-love: consciousness and concentration on someone else.

So long as we are in contact with the objectified, we may be egocentric and unconscious, since we ourselves are absorbed by the process of objectifying (an essentially egoistic function) and are yet unconscious of spiritual energy as such.

But at adolescence, it is the contact with energy that takes precedence over all else. We interrupt objectification and revise its energetic content, retrieving what was in excess, setting things in order and preparing the way for a freer spiritual life. No longer having to concentrate on the creation of action patterns which are now available and tested, we can take a most immediate step, delayed until now by necessity: we can feel ourselves continuously and not only incidentally as before.

Our contact with others exists and in definite patterns. We do not yet know enough of what we are to modify our feelings towards our relatives; our feelings will only be revised as we discover what makes us human. This discovery is not intellectual, it is direct knowledge of ourselves as energy. Often a painful discovery, it is anyway so profoundly overwhelming that it transforms our whole life (as we shall try to describe in chapter 5). In order to re-establish our confidence we project ourselves onto someone else living the same experience, we choose a friend for ourselves, in general from our own environment but outside the family. We create links with our new self—but in the friend. This is why we do not become moralists. Since we do not yet know the qualities of spiritual energy, we shall discover them in the other one, as he will in us. We certainly go on enlightening ourselves with the help of our former vision, but not exclusively and less and less. Instead of attachment-love we shall know friendship.

The inevitability of the link with others will be replaced by a choice and by reciprocation; demands by tolerance. The search for what can unite us further will be the object of all our efforts, and we shall slowly forget the blackmail procedures which are effective in attachment-love. We shall love someone for his own sake. We shall learn to project onto him our ideal; we shall learn to adorn him with what we shall discover to be present potentially in spiritual energy, the one which animates us and which we cannot yet analyze. In objectifying these powers we get a better hold on them. In attributing them to someone, we prove the existence of spiritual energy. In perceiving its presence in the friend we reach the truth with regard to it. Our capacity for infinite gift is a trait of the infinite possibility of our self, but the present tenuous contact with energy does not allow us yet to be sure of it. The habit of objectifying makes us place it outside ourselves: objectively in someone.

Thus attachment-love matures into friendship. The first is full of frustrations and contradictions, and our friendship will try to be free of them. We only knew how to receive and did not know the meaning of the act of giving, although this word was used by those who said they were giving to us. Now there is no need to go outside ourselves in order to understand it, no more need for an act of the imagination. We can experience it within. The free nature of the gift is its new merit, its spontaneity, its authenticity. We experience in ourselves what our egocentricism prevented us from feeling: we become conscious, not of that which will remain for long still unconscious, but of the creation of affective links, of the creation in ourselves of a place for someone else, of the establishing in our affectivity of a new living image of the one whom we have chosen to keep in our heart. This friend will live in us, of us. Someone separate is thus integrated, and has the freedom of moving within us, to be himself and yet intimately ours. This harmony, this new love, is friendship.

Our relations have no longer the nostalgic character so frequent in attachment liaisons. The ideal is not what previously existed but that which is to come. With the friend it is not the past which counts, there is none; it is the projection into the future, it is the temporal adventure, lived together, far from those who have a "right" to us and our affections. It is the conquest, we know not of what, but the concerted, accepted conquest, the spiritual conquest first and foremost—of love, of God, of the whole future. The friend is distinct from the parents because with him we leave the realm of the objectified, the known, the established, conformity, and therefore we undertake the possible and the impossible (we do not yet distinguish them), the unknown, the revolutionary, the new. The friend is the witness of the changes which we hide from all, and, in giving ourselves in all confidence, we know that we run no danger since he surrenders as much of himself to us and we experience each other as if we were a single being.

Friendship-love accomplishes the metamorphosis of attachment-love into a love which is potentially universal.

In fact, universal love alone has a right to be qualified as love. Love is not attachment, and it is not the result of a choice as in friendship. It is this that the great masters who are the saints of all religions and all ages tell us about true love. This love—universal love—seems to be an exception and only exceptional people seem capable of experiencing it. It is generally thought that a special grace is necessary in order to experience it, and its presence is attributed to the presence of God in the saint. In my opinion and in the opinion of those who have experienced it, however, it is not at all a supernatural phenomenon. It is our spirituality, I believe, which explains it, and it is this also which makes it possible. It is because we do not recognize ourselves as spiritual beings that the only love we ordinarily know is attachment-love with some glimmers in friendship.

Let us consider the spirituality, the affectivity in which we have just seen a friend living. Is not this friend, up to a certain point, indeterminate? Is it he who determines the image that represents him to our eyes? Or are we in some way included in it also? Obviously the two things work on each other and, in so far as it is we who animate the being that we have separated in us, we are responsible for our love while we leave the recipient indeterminate. We thus enter universal love.

Since friendship-love is the gift of oneself to someone who lives in us, freely, entirely, with his rights and characteristics, it means that there is room in us for other people who may live our life. It cannot be the structure of the friend that dwells in us since we are separated nor can it be his image since he is allowed to be himself. It must be that which embraces the structure, that which inhabits it intimately. It is by means of it that we suffer for our friend, and by which we communicate with him; it is by it that we are linked, united with him. It is that which can emanate from one and invade the other. It is that which is an ideal, by reason of all the unobjectified possibilities. This is the future, this is hope and love. By means of it we learn through friendship-love to give ourselves, to prepare ourselves for the other one, for the friend. But if we limit ourselves to a single being, we may find that we have replaced friendship-love by attachment-love, that we have returned to egocentricity and unconsciousness.

True universal love is friendship-love multiplied a hundred fold, made absolutely free, open to all, ready for all, for everyone. One does not love the whole of humanity as one loves a friend. One loves humans, not all humans as a fact, but each one who comes. Universal love is a universal possibility of loving. As soon as the person to be loved appears, there is a place for him. A place ready made, as if it had always been waiting. Just the right place. He does not know if this place has been prepared for him. He accepts it. He recognizes it as his own, it is his, completely. He who loves universally seems to await encounters. Why this one rather than that one? Everyone has a right to his love and everyone accepts the place he offers without demanding anything in return, as with a friend. Reciprocity alone gives the right to remain there.

He who loves universally knows that all is possible with him, that his affectivity can be shared between each of his human brothers. In him all men are strong. All ages, all deformities, all frustrations, all joys. In him pre-exist all the combinations of behavior each of which constitutes a man. The one whom he loves finds himself at ease with him, as with a friend, since he is entirely welcomed, without possible restrictions because of his qualities or faults, his gifts or injuries of any kind. The one whom he loves does not know why it is that he feels so much at home with the other. And this feeling of security, of perfect harmony assures him that it is love which he is offered and not attachment, a gift which is given and not a loan. The one who loves does not lend. What's more, he even makes no gift, he becomes the other one, and this state suffices to create all that friendship gives: an experience of warmth, of presence, of human presence merging on divine presence—that is to say: a universal experience.

In fact, there cannot simultaneously be universal love and participation—that affective adhesion, conscious or not, to a scheme, a thought, a rite, an object, an organization, which makes the subject feel himself a part of the scheme, thought, etc. (Participation is therefore the psychological phenomenon by which one penetrates the elements of the natural and social universe by making over a part of oneself to it.) Participation is a residue of attachment, a statification of affectivity, therefore a lack of availability with regard to the one who comes or the next one to whom one will give everything, as is his due. A perfect availability is a corollary of universal love, and it is not possible unless nonparticipation is attained.

Now it is possible to educate for nonparticipation. The means to make it attainable for those who seek it are already known. Therefore education for love is possible, and we must now speak of it.

It is evident from the start that education for love will not be possible until we have an adequate number of adults capable of completely liberating themselves from attachment-love in order to arrive at a kind of affective detachment. The consciousness of their spirituality and of their partial freedom will permit them to consider themselves as something other than being determined by their affective traumatisms. They will next be able to become parents and to consider the affective life of their children in its true perspective and not lose sight of the affective freedom which experience creates. Attachment-love will not be the only love resulting from family life.

If the parental love is well balanced and spiritualized as much as it can be, the children will be led by the exercise of autonomy to become successively aware of the gratuitousness of a gift and of its value for the individual who receives it. The child, who cannot avoid being egocentric at the beginning, can, following appropriate active and affective exercises, be detached from his central position and attain a relative position, like that spontaneously attained in large families where harmony reigns. There, each child assumes his position of elder brother for his younger brothers and all are included in the social life of the family. Everyone, at every age level, receives and gives according to his ability and means, and the numerous preoccupations arising in communal living prevent him from concentrating on his pseudo-problems. It is obviously not always thus in large families, but the favorable conditions I have described have more chance of arising there than in families with an only child, where this child is almost inevitably the center of its parental affective life. In any case, it seems essential that attachment-love be countered and not accentuated as certain psychologists insist. Children need love, but not false love which will make them unhappy. If the child be weak, he needs care and help. But what he needs above everything else is autonomy as a preparation for the future. He demands love as a source of liberation and not of slavery, and attachment-love is a very strong form of slavery.

As soon as the child enters into contact with his affectivity, during adolescence,* he must be encouraged to make friends (one friend at first), for as long as he remains at this stage, then education must lead him to understand his capacity for friendship, of love for all.

My experience—as one who was an adolescent and as an observer of adolescents—makes me utterly confident that, from the age of fifteen or sixteen years, the adolescent is capable of the highest things that life has to offer him. Universal love inspires him much more than attachment-love, and if he meets examples of universal love, he is won by it and desires to experience it in his turn.

The road to achieving nonparticipation is more difficult. Here I must speak with a personalness not at all customary in works that aim at general propositions. But since we learn all things only by ourselves, from our own experience, I can present my experience as an authentic example of what can be done, possibly valid for all.

I have succeeded in creating, experimentally, multiple solid friendships, which capability may extend to others. I believe that in such friendships, and with the

---

*In the following chapters we study this moment in detail. However, a cautionary note on the affectivity of the younger child is in order here. I believe that the affectivity of the younger child is still unconscious but that it is none the less real for being unconscious. It is even more vulnerable. Because of this, it raises numerous important questions, but these cannot be discussed in this book, centered on adolescence.

knowledge of spirituality, we are able to detach ourselves totally from attachment and to penetrate nonparticipating universal love. I, and others, have seen the taste for friendship be born and flourish in adolescents, and have seen the gift of giving oneself, a priori, to those with whom we are going to live happily and abundantly a rich affective experience. I have been able to assure myself that it is possible to avoid the risk of missing love when replacing superficial sentiments by nonparticipation. It is the attachment which we try to eliminate, not love, the self-attachment of egocentricism, the attachment to friends that one once had. I propose firm friendships, which renew themselves and multiply, which grow as we conquer our spirituality. The warmth of friendship does not disappear in universal love except for those who want to attach, fix, rivet the one who gives, be it in the form of love, or in a preconceived framework of what is true love; that is to say, for one who has not been able to go beyond attachment-love.

What of filial love? Jesus said to his mother, "Woman what requirest thou of me?" All the saints left their families or, as Saint Bernard did, led some of its members to a monastery where a new relationship was established between them; attachment may be overthrown.

Spiritual love is not what is called platonic love, which may perfectly well be sensual attachment to an image. Spiritual love is giving, softness and warmth, and not possession, even imagined. In the one case, the one who loves brings to the loved one all that can comfort and exalt him; in the other, he imposes his ways, his outlook, his vision. In the first an adequate presence is offered, in the second, no presence is possible.

Spiritual love does not exclude sexual love, but in it, contrary to what our age has wished to codify, the sexual function is not isolated, lived in itself. It is precisely one of the consequences of attachment-love (which science has tried to uplift and justify) that the loved one is loved for one's pleasure, one's joy, and becomes an element in one's psychic and vegetative life. As such, this type of love enters into the cycle of psychic functions (common to animals and sexed plants), and the already egocentric and unconscious links which govern this love expand in the functions. In the process we smother those we love with attachment, we need their presence, the pressure of their hand, their caresses. But for those whom we love in friendship or spiritually, our attentions are more subtle, more delicate, better appreciated.

Attachment-love leads to biological functions. Sexuality becomes separated and cultivated for itself, as a special function. It has been thus at all times, and every civilization has had its own customs. In ours, more than in any other, the separation has been pushed very far, and the cultivation of sexuality has passed into the mores under the heading of preparation for love, for a harmonious conjugal life. In some schools sex education has been adopted, but there is still no question of education for love unless love is confused with sexuality, as so often happens. The isolated sexual function no longer inspires fear. On the contrary, it is thought that its free consideration protects us from the dangers of repression, that it has right of place, and it is a step forward to make it more and more conscious and felt.

Is not that another of our mistakes?

Let us not misunderstand this remark. I do not intend to attack the sexual function through prudery or prejudice. It is, I believe, the conception of complete health that I have suggested in this discussion which alerts us to the danger of the current extreme emphasis on the sexual function.

First of all, the sexual function is not a function except for those who wish to isolate it and study it separately. It is a part of our integral life and, except for the purpose of analysis, cannot be further isolated than the function carried out by our feet. Sexuality in connection with reproduction, which is a vital function, only exists in animals. Man has at all times separated love and the reproductive function. He is capable of the sex act whatever the state of impregnation of his partner may be. He has removed the seasons of copulation, he has discovered since Onan (and no doubt before) the means to avoid conception, carried to a high degree of perfection today. Impregnation is a social problem and no longer a biological one.

Thus, man and woman can indulge in all the fantasies in the art of sexual play. But, and this is the point, they can equally well be chaste. They cannot, however, stop their hearts or their respiration. Circulation, respiration are biological functions; in man sexuality is not. It becomes so following a decision of the mind, a decision often taken by the group and which results in conceptions born of attachment-love and its train of demands and conventions. Science today, which isolates and studies the vicissitudes of attachment-love, has been the victim of a preference for an ideal, according to which man has been considered at the most as a psychic being, having only biological energy.

But if one knows that man is a spiritual being all is different and love no longer means to possess. In the sexual union of two people who love each other spiritually, there is a total giving without seeking, not special concentration on pleasure, a gift of one to the other, without biological or psychical ends. Sexual love for man is neither good nor bad, nor an act to be done in isolation, nor a way to procreate or preserve the species. Man, as a spiritual being, transcended primitive determinism when he realized that the sex act in him is different from that of animals. He transcended in the process the sense of sin attached to the conception of the body as an inferior part of the person. And he transcended the exaltation of the modern disciples of Bacchus and the psychoanalysts in discovering that there was nothing necessary or definitive in his sexual experience. He simply considers sexual acts as elements of love when this is really spiritualized, as the fusion of affectivities, and he does not place sex and love on different hierarchical planes.

Chaste love for those who find their religious symbolisms demanding it, sexual love for those who are masters of themselves—such are the forms of spiritual love lived by spiritual people. Physical love separated from love is one of the anomalies which man meets when he has lost his knowledge of himself as a spiritual being.

To educate for love comes back to the necessity of making the spiritual nature of the whole human person known to all.* The rest follows naturally.

—————

*I have omitted a discussion of education for charity because it raises new psychosociological and historic questions which require other ideas and ways of approach. But I think that such an education is not entirely alien to what has been discussed in this chapter.

4.   On Inspiration, Spiritual Contagion and Brotherhood

WE have seen how affectivity permeates objectifications and is part of the total energy which will be recognized at a given moment as such; how the discovery of "the other" is a special act of our spirituality, a becoming aware that some others are spiritual beings with whom we may have spiritual relations. We have seen that these others live in our affectivity. Their gestures are familiar to us, whether it be a question of language, of ritual symbolism, or of personal gestures. This familiarity is equivalent to their life in us.

Now we must add to this portrait of our spirituality. Already before our conscious recognition of others, we were deeply engaged in spiritual dialogues with the universe, of which we were not necessarily conscious and for whose nature I will use the word contagion, spiritual influence. Then, after the recognition of the existence of others, we are engaged in a new dialogue, conscious this time, which is still of the spiritual contagion type, but whose mechanism is different; we shall call it (with the psychologist J. E.

Marcault) the law of Spiritual Brotherhood, and note that it is also the law of inspiration.

The turning point between contagion (unconscious) and brotherhood (conscious) is the turning from objectification without spiritual awareness to internal objectification of one's conscious spirituality (in various forms). Adolescence is the period of this turning point when contagion and potential fraternity are co-present.

The psychology of contagion follows the course taken by our general spiritual evolution. Thus, as long as we are in the process of objectifying, it is from the domain of objectifications that we shall form a hierarchy of spiritual influences. At the height of our capacity for objectification, we place the person who to us objectifies most and best. It is certainly we who create this peak and who place thereon such or such a person, but once the person is there, he leads us to an objectification nearer his own and one that is potentially possible for us because it is the result of our projection. The whole way in which sports inspire is contagion of this sort. The symbolism contained in the figures "100 yards in 9 4/5 sec." is capable of engaging in affectivity of numbers of young men to the point where they impose on themselves very severe disciplines in order that they themselves as well as the champion succeed in reaching this achievement—objectifying their ability—on the track. This power of contagion is inherent in our affectivity and in the fact that man is capable of all behaviors. One man is moved by physical performances, another by social successes, another by intellectual performances—but all are responding to elements from the domain of objectification. The symbolism of contagion is varied. A job behind a counter, the activity of being a train driver, the possession of a sack of crowns, or of a piano, etc. are sources of contagion and of potential liberation for the mechanisms of objectification which enable us to achieve the objectification in question.

Spiritual contagion governs the relationship between individuals who objectify. It is the expression of this relationship and, through our lives, operates on this level. When a child has established action mechanisms, he is ready to make use of them, and does so, guided by contagion. His parents have a mastery of action completely different from his, and they appear to him as the peak of his powers of objectification. His companions, brothers and schoolmates, may be between the two, when they objectify better than he, which differences he can recognize by his own appreciation of both his performances and theirs. When he too excels in whatever he has undertaken, and now serves as a source of contagion, he himself (during this state) does not experience pride, he simply acts as a source for others because he does well. The imitator is drawn to the model, but not conversely. Furthermore, the power of contagion from one to another is lost as soon as the objectification is effected; as soon as the pupil has as much mastery as his teacher, in general the latter can no longer affect him. The former model may even be criticized and removed from the pedestal where he had been placed, often without knowing it or being consulted.

Spiritual contagion functions amidst behavior, in things and ideas. But it can only function under certain conditions.

Firstly, there can be contagion only between people capable of similar objectifications and only with regard to behaviors that the individual perceives as being objectified. Thus, a young child may cry because his hero gets into a dangerous situation, while this same situation fills his older brothers with enthusiasm. Similarly, for a believer, a religious monument is full of meaning but can only be an object for an unbeliever. In both these cases, for a movement to occur in the affectivity of individuals— for contagion to take place—there must be a relationship to the individual's power to objectify, conveyed either by greater experience (as with the older boy) or because one has a cultural "entry" into a situation (as with the believer).

Next, there can only be contagion when the range of the objectifications is such that the person stimulated knows that the behavior which attracts him is accessible to him. A mathematical proposition leaves someone unmoved until he knows its meaning, then he may be transported with joy.

Contagion is not therefore automatic, and it has its own laws. But it is automatic within the framework which its laws impose. No one is conscious of inducing contagion or of responding to it if the act of living takes place spontaneously. Spiritual contagion envelops us like air. It is everywhere in the universe because we come into the world with the power to objectify but not all at the same level with regard to the same behaviors, and this variance operates as an attraction towards the higher levels. One who has objectified normally serves as a source, as a model for someone who has not yet reached the same level, and induces affective currents in the other which lead him to a similar objectification.

It is curious that objects can lead us immediately to determined behaviors: certain statues force some people to kneel and others to experience an aesthetic emotion, while they leave others indifferent. The existence of people who themselves make clay objects and place them on an altar and then address a prayer to them, shows us that the power of objects is not the result of education or the environment alone, but that a strong individual spiritual element exists in the action of objects on the spirit. The primitive's clay was animated by a form which seemed to him capable of subordinating matter to it. The life of the forms which the primitive invokes is in fact (as in all such cases) his own dynamism which will, perhaps, act again, on other elements of life. (There is a difference between the object's power and our belief, only because we believe the form to be buried, dead in the clay, while for the primitive it animates the clay.)

The whole universe is thus successively inhabited by the spirit. Is there any difference between the action of a music manuscript on a musician and that of a statue on a believer? It is not sufficient to be able to read the notes, as it is not sufficient to be able to look at the statue. One must be an initiate; one must have objectified in a certain way, in order to grasp the living meaning of each. When one empties the manuscript and the statue of their true spiritual life, both become equivalent objects and of little value. It is in so far as the universe is spiritual that it is capable of inspiring men. Just as for the physicist it is cosmic energy that acts according to its laws of omnipresence, so for the psychologist the universe is filled with our human presence which acts according to its spiritual laws upon the men who make the universe, live it and relive it.

Up to now we have avoided speaking of the action

of energy on energy, and we have limited ourselves to contagion and the action of behaviors. We did refer to a hierarchy in the capacity of people to influence each other, but we avoided the selection of a particular hierarchy. Now that we must deal with spiritual action as such this is no longer possible, and the hierarchy becomes necessary by the nature of things. While we left the order of contagion indefinite in order to describe contagion in general, it is no longer the same when attempting to give a complete picture of spiritual action from birth to death for the individual and from its constitution to its dissolution for civilizations.

We have spoken of contagion as an unconscious phenomenon. Now we shall call the conscious phenomenon *inspiration.*

The word "admire" and the pneumatic origin of the words "aspire" and "inspire" indicate that there is a hierarchy between the people participating in the act in question. I admire, I look afar, towards something. I aspire, that inspires me—these are complementary acts where a close connection is visible. If that inspires me, it envelops me. If I aspire to it, it means that I am on the way to attaining it. Therefore, for the inspired, the inspirer is greater and the hierarchy is spontaneously constituted by him. There is no longer any question about it, a fact is recognized: this inspires me and I aspire to it.

Admiration then appears as the subject's awareness that he is inspired and that he aspires. In admiration, there is a source which elevates and a person who is elevated. *The source is always spiritual.* When it is a question of objects, of landscapes, contagion has been the work of a consciousness which has perceived the spiritual content of the object or the landscape. For proof, it is sufficient to recall that, in the Western civilization, it was during the Romantic Era that man filled nature with what today it seems to contain naturally. In comparing the landscape, as described by two writers of the seventeenth and nineteenth centuries or as pictured by two painters from the same periods, it will be understood that the spiritualization of objects comes from the person who projects himself into it and succeeds in moving his contemporaries—that is, convinces them that this new quality he recognizes is so.

It was the descriptions of the Romantics, who cultivated the feeling of nature, which gave the power of inspiration to a nature that had possessed it in but small measure before. But even in this new general feeling for nature one finds large gaps. A highly sensitive person who responds to forests and lakes may remain unmoved in the presence of glaciers whose aesthetic power of inspiration remains to be discovered.

This being so, we may in this discussion, without fear of error, consider only spiritual energies in action, and not concern ourselves with the particular objectification of these energies. It will be the effects of the one, the source, on the other, the subject, which will be described (whether these effects are brought out in a form or are free).

If, for various reasons, we were to neglect the influences of contagion described above (which nonetheless operate throughout life), then we would still need to try to understand the phenomenon known by the name of conversion. All those who have undergone a normal amount of social traumatisms and whom life has not too sparsely endowed with opportunity have had this experience—that is to say, nearly everyone. Conversion is the spiritual phenom-enon in which we abruptly come face to face with a part of ourselves or of the spiritual universe in us, which up to now we had not known. A conversion is not necessarily final or unique. It is final when it permits a reorganization of all our affectivity; it renews itself when other reorganizations are possible. Sometimes, after one conversion, one attains energy as such, and there is no longer any question of reorganizing their affectivity, instead there is direct use of energy.

When conversion takes place, it always follows on an abrupt awareness that we are in a spiritually determined universe, even though we may use other terms to characterize this awareness. But there is a sense that something in the universe is absolutely so and that this determination is imposed by a (spiritual) being who inspires us and whose message bears the sign of truth, making us feel completely certain. Conversion always occurs within another experience, within the experience of our inspirer, to whose power we have completely surrendered and who imposes on us his symbolism and his experience as a whole. If this is limited, our experience may exceed it; the inspirer is then rejected, overtaken, and a new conversion becomes possible. If it is limitless for us, we may grow in it all our life, and we will not cease to admire it as effectively. We shall always aspire higher in order to identify ourselves with it. It will remain our ideal, our inspirer. Such are the lives of Jesus, or Buddha, or Mohammed, for their disciples. Such are not the adventures in Western movies or the experience of Hitler or Mussolini who have, however, inspired millions of young minds.

The mechanism of inspiration is now clear. An

aspiration exists in us, created by an inspiration, and we place this inspiration in a person, we project it beyond ourselves, giving our spiritual life the impetus which will lead us, as spiritual beings, to relive the life of our inspirer (or rather his experience as we understand it) and to familiarize ourselves either with his objectifications or with the ways he acts upon—uses—his spiritual energy. We are one person becoming another. At a certain natural and spontaneous altitude, which is his own, the presence of the inspirer places our spiritual energy in a state of aspiration from which come the spiritual acts that result in our elevation. The inspirer needs only to be what he is, convincingly.

The state of tension of our spiritual energy (often confused with affectivity) is what polarizes this energy.

The pervading presence of the inspirer is translated into a transcendental mechanism for the inspired person, a continuous growth which makes successive levels recede until active energy is reached. This growth increases, leaning on itself, but at the same time reaching out towards an immanent spiritual state attributed to the inspirer; it continually expands and transcends itself. As long as aspiration and inspiration are active, they find possibilities which they did not have in the beginning, either on the plane of objectification or on the plane of spiritual energy itself (that is to say, spiritual energy not statified in objectifications).

It often happens, as we have noted can happen in contagion, that this transcendence rapidly results in the destruction of all the inspirer's prestige. Every day we are faced with objects which we have admired and which have lost their power of inspiration and leave us indifferent or which we even scorn. This happens, for example, in the simple physical growth which at first makes us admire powers in our parents, a superiority they lose as we grow in our powers—and sometimes do better than those who once transcended us. Our schoolmasters suffer a similar fate intellectually.

This brings us to two questions, that of the hierarchy in one life and those of the hierarchies in different civilizations. The second we shall not examine in the present discussion. For our purposes here, we shall limit ourselves to a single aspect of the first which does not involve the second.

We have seen that spiritual contagion is only possible when the spiritual distance between the inspirer and the inspired is not too great concerning the objectification in question. Therefore, by reason of this law, it seems that the power of the inspirer will only operate over a short period and that it will inevitably be transcended. This is the case in the lives of a multitude of inspirers, particularly on the physical and intellectual planes (though even on these planes there exists many examples of inspirers having maintained their power for a very long time).

In general, inspirers may be subdivided into those whose power is temporary, those whose power renews itself, and finally those whose power is permanent. The mechanism of their action is always the same. But those whom they inspire are able to transcend the experience of the first, to always find new reasons for admiration in the second, and to never cease being inspired by the last. In general, the first inspire without wishing to and only because their objectifications surpass those of others. The second we may call the *Elder Brothers,* which is the aspect of hierarchy we will discuss here, and the third the *Masters.*

The Elder Brothers are aware that they have the function of inspiration to fulfill, and they consciously look for the means to do it. They know that their experience must be of such quality that it renews itself in contact with those who must be led to the transcendence of this experience. They know that their freedom consists in the power of living more intensely and on a higher plane than those they inspire, so that a polarization of the experience of others results. Their freedom is not an absolute freedom but a freedom conscious of what it entails. Freedom is necessary to Elder Brothers so that their experience be authentic, and it must be a freeing that results from a liberation from their dependencies and unconscious participations, that results from love. The Elder Brother loves and takes his place in the hierarchy of the family of Elder Brothers, beneath those of whom he has need for his own development, above those who need him in order to develop. If he continues to grow, he, by this means, renews himself as a source of inspiration. In this process, the law of brotherhood which governs inspiration and spiritual contagion becomes conscious.

While spiritual contagion operates within its own framework automatically, the law of brotherhood only functions through the consciousness of the Elder Brothers. It is their responsibility which creates it. Love is their driving power and their *raison d'être* to help lift the energy of the younger to the highest levels of awareness and realization, the levels of the Masters. If they refuse to do it, the law of brotherhood would cease to operate. Love would have to create other paths leading directly to the Masters, who through this renewal generate new Elder Brothers such as have never been lacking on the earth and in all civilizations. The law of brotherhood becomes effective because some men take the responsibility of serving as a bridge between the greatest and the smallest in spiritual experience. Because they devote themselves to this end, their lives become a source of inspiration and their actions are out of the ordinary. They acquire the characteristics of Elder Brothers by their actions, which may be heroic or humble, but always conscious, which are retained and repeated and which polarize the will, the affectivity of those who will grow by means of them.

There is no typical approach for the Elder Brother in his action on the younger ones. But this action makes certain demands. It must emanate from authentic experience; it must be strong and lasting; it must be present in the affectivity and, by it, enlighten the intellect and action itself. It must be its own proof and not seek any justification. At this price it becomes activating. It is like a source of spiritual radio-elements, "artificially" produced by spontaneously active elements, but "radioactive" all the same and only "artificial" when one knows their source. The law of brotherhood assures us of the result without allowing us to say more than this: human beings are all susceptible to inspiration; this truth is manifested in making the inspired inspirers in their own turn, and so on. The chain is established.

Where does it begin and where finish?

This question is of the second hierarchy and we shall say no more about it now.

To sum up: in our discussion, I have distinguished spiritual contagion from the law of inspiration (the law of brotherhood) in order to emphasize that the first functions by means of energy more or less organized and operates on affectivity, while the second operates on the available free energy and, contrary to objectifications, leads to the greater liberation of the individual towards the superior spiritual destinies realized by the Masters.

5.   The Psychology of Adolescence

WE come now to adolescence. On several occasions I have presented my definition of adolescence. It is that period of spiritual life when the self recognizes itself as energy and perceives itself as something beyond its objectifications and the function of objectifying. It sees that it is more than just its behaviors and the process by which it brings these behaviors into being. It sees itself as a participant in a dynamic spiritual universe.

This definition is at least as good as any other. Also it has several advantages of which the most important is that it does not force one to consider the psyche first in examining the adolescent. It is a definition which agrees with a psychology of awareness. Basically, its outcome will prove its usefulness.

The recognition that forms the core of the definition—the recognition by the self that it can go beyond objectification—is not intellectual. It is, on the contrary, the point of departure of what will become the intellect (in the sense of mind in seventeenth century philosophy), as we shall see later. To recognize oneself as energy is to become aware of what is in us outside of objectifications, and this new awareness is precisely what takes place in the revision of the content of his "soul" which the adolescent undertakes. While in the preceding period every child only objectified his means of action, which were experienced as awareness of action itself, now the individual examines his actions with regard to their energy content; it is in this change that we see the fundamental difference between the general behavior of the boy or girl and that of the young man or young woman that is immediately visible to all.

In particular, the adolescent's search for solitude and his increased sensitivity to pain, whether it be of physical or mental origin, emphasizes this difference. Memory becomes a much more active and conscious function; this happens because it is concerned with affectivity and the inner life. (Some psychologists speak of "affective memory," but there is no other kind, unless we look only at automatisms, at objectifications organized for perfect automatic action within an affectivity not yet aware of itself.)

In relation to behavior, there are many indications proving the contact of the self with itself, at first in the form of affectivity, and then as free spiritual energy. We shall leave to our readers to study this, the central point having been made. Here, we shall try to explain two important phenomena in the life of the adolescent; the discovery of religion and of thought— because these are indeed discoveries, even if the child has lived immersed in a religious life in the social meaning of the word. (Religion, it is true, is not always available to the child, but the process that leads to religion always is, so for the moment we shall let the discovery of religion stand for this process.)

As we said earlier, each child finds "natural" and "social" elements mixed in his environment and only distinguishes them very slowly. In animating nature, he proves to us that for him there is only one world, but these two elements will be more or less separated according to the civilization in which a child is born. He finds therefore in his environment religious rites, objectifications of beliefs, moral rules in operation, and he learns to fear taboos, as well as fire or vertigo. His growth in the environment leads him to distinguish, for example, the meaning of words from the words themselves, such as he hears them and reads them; but it also leads him to see the physical and moral worlds related. (He is also forced to this realization by such things as the beating which he may receive in punishment for certain types of behavior.)

The discovery that there are two worlds, the world of nature and the world of men, is a very slow and sometimes painful process. This discovery becomes possible only for someone at the threshold of self-awareness, when self-awareness isolates him from the rest of creation and when, on the other hand, friendship secures him against loneliness. In fact the two experiences, that there is a self and there is a world, occur at adolescence as spiritual experiences. The separation of oneself from creation suppresses animism and places us in a position of spatial relativism. We recognize ourselves, through our bodies, as a part of and in submission to, laws shared by things. But this corporeal separation and this spatial relativism pre-suppose that we have ceased the objectification of action and are about to become aware of a spiritual duality which was unknown until then.

This becoming aware is double in appearance. One recognizes oneself as energy and objectification at the same time. But while the objectification aspect is still very familiar, the energy aspect is entirely new to the adolescent, and from this contact with something new amid the familiar results a feeling of duality which at the outset is very disturbing. The contact with energy brings us back to ourselves—to a self, unknown, but which familiarly continues through the acquired momentum of living in objectification and the objectified. This manifestation of the unknown amid the familiar pulls us up short, leads us to enter more deeply into contact with ourselves, and makes us confer directly with our affectivity. To ask affective questions to which there are only affective answers. The answers will enter the realm of the objectified, become objective in the friend who goes through the same experience. But neither of the friends has a reply other than that of affectivity, which is more and more manifestly present as our questioning becomes more precise, more "educated." Life becomes an affective life.

Emerging slowly above the other functions which are still active, affectivity gets more attention from the self and begins to be organized within it making use of the spiritual energy recognized in the self and in the objectifications. From these, the self abstracts any energy that is found to have been put in them in excess of what was necessary for their proper functioning. This recuperated energy plus the energy accessible in affectivity itself can now be used directly, and it animates the whole spiritual universe encountered in the heretofore unconscious objectification.

In particular, in the rituals of the immediate environment the self finds a new inspiration. This is why the adolescent discovers not God but the god of his religion, the god of the symbolism that he has invested in his objectifications, which are those of his environment and which he has not questioned during the former period of his life because he was completely absorbed by the task of creating for himself the frameworks of action.

The discovery of religion is therefore nothing less than the discovery of spiritual energy, but in the only form that it can take in the adolescent who can only analyze his objectifications: the religion of his environment. But it is still discovered as a spiritual life because we abundantly clothe it with spirituality. These objectifications will gather new truth, will become a true source of inspiration because they are now spiritualized—and the adolescent is ready to give them the power that symbolism has placed in them. Thus we discover the god of a religion (if the religion of the environment possesses one), and at the same time, discover the whole of our religion. We feel that all those who belong to it are brothers, and we find, in the saints and the officiating priests, Masters and Elder Brothers who are capable of acting on our spiritual energy through the symbolism of the religion and to lead us still nearer to the heart of the religion. We find that the only path which will lead us to become growing spiritual beings is that which the symbolism of our religion offers us. The more we discover our spirituality, the more we are caught up in symbolism, which then acquires such an absolute character that we are led to identify spirituality and religious experience within the framework of our particular religious symbolism.

Everywhere the adolescent is the victim of this spiritual mechanism whereby he identifies religion and spirituality, and when religion is lacking (because the parents are atheists or the environment has excluded it), he makes it reappear by allowing himself to be converted or by proposing his own atheism as an absolute, or by using any political or other belief which is offered him with sufficient conviction.

It is first in himself that the adolescent discovers religion because he discovers there his own spiritual energy. He then considers as *the* religion the one which his environment offers him. We can say therefore that all men are religious because it is their destiny to recognize themselves as spiritual energy at the end of their objectification; they do not all belong to a single religion, although each adolescent goes through the same experience, because man objectifies amid a given spiritual contagion and because various symbolisms have been propounded in the world.

If the contact with energy is direct and total, it may happen that the adolescent transcends one symbolism and discovers another, but this is so rare that the phenomenon can only be referred to as a theoretical possibility. Cases of spontaneous conversion from one religion to another do exist even though in the environment there existed only the possibility of knowing one of them. Saint Paul would more or less symbolize this case, Uriel da Costa realized it.

At the same time as the adolescent discovers religion, he is organizing his affectivity. This means that he consciously builds affective categories for himself. In his solitude, he is able to experience all degrees of sorrow, joy, pleasure, nervous exhaustion, exaltation, tension, etc. He achieves internal recognition of similarities and nuances and of a profoundly *felt* classification which forms an affective substructure and will serve as a basis for the future. Emotions are analytically experienced and feelings are constituted as frameworks for these emotions, thus forming affective categories, which then are "abstractly" objectified.

The becoming aware of a feeling and of the emotions which compose it, it should be made clear, is not the becoming aware of an objectification. When the child coordinated his perceptions to undertake an action, he created a multidimensional image which was organized, statified energy. Now, the emotions are recognized wherever they are found as forming a feeling—anger, joy, sorrow, etc.—not because the feeling is organized energy but because the energy itself is recognized as being in a characteristic state of tension. It is, in other words, a spiritual state and not an organization of the energy.

The formation of feelings is possible at adolescence because this is the period of life when contact with energy takes place. What takes place previously in regard to affectivity may be explained, as in the case of attachment-love, by the interplay of the unconscious and egocentric necessity of the child's life. Psychoanalysis furnishes us with numerous examples of unconscious "feelings" obscured by the action of consciousness and eliminated from the domain of complexes (which is a more fitting word). In adolescence, feelings are consciously created, and they constitute a framework not only for affective and moral life as I already have implied, but also for intellectual life.

It may be useful, by way of contrast, to note that Piaget also recognizes that logical analytic intelligence is reached in adolescence. But there are fundamental differences between his view of its appearance and the view offered here. Piaget offers a genetic interpretation of intelligence, but I believe that the rudimentary forms of intellectual analysis which he finds in childhood have no connections with the finished forms he finds, except for the connections which he himself introduces.

As long as a child objectifies, his knowledge of mechanisms included in perception and action is intimately linked with and grounded in the act of living at this level. For the child, there is a *perceptive-active* logic, an *active* philosophy, an *active* theology, etc. When he ceases objectifying and discovers himself as energy, the adolescent shows that he can no longer use a logic (except that of action, which already exists and comes into play when he acts). His intelligence cannot be defined through the analysis of actions or situations. He has no measurable intelligence in the sense in which the intelligence of children or adults has been measured, as the failure of all attempts to test it at this age prove. Since his intelligence is affective and so is to be defined by *the analysis of emotions and the constitution of feelings* (states of tension of active energy), it will have its own dynamics, and while creating the abstract categories of feelings and sentiments (which action cannot do and which language does only for the grown-up adult), it allows the establishment of the true dynamics abstracted from the entire context of the objectifications.

As adolescents discover their religion in their

spiritual energy mixed with the objectifications, they discover Thought (the thought of their time) in their language, the categories of feelings serving as frameworks for the known conceptual categories, used but not yet fully understood. At this point the adolescent freely thinks his own thoughts. He has, for the first time, an intellectual logic which comes from and codifies the mechanism of action of which he has become aware and which is rendered real through the categories of feelings. Action and affectivity with its dynamics together give birth to thought per se which is dynamic, because it is active, and which integrates all the possibilities of action experienced so far in active life plus the possibilities that the freedom of the self give it. It is because energy reaches itself that thought can become aware of itself and be recognized as true independently from logic (which thought proves rather than the reverse). Logic which is the mechanism of thinking, appears as a residue of the mechanism of action activated by affectivity; it adds nothing to intellectual life, it only defines one of its aspects.

Intellectual life is spiritual life—on the one hand because it derives from affectivity and on the other, because it represents a new possibility of spiritual energy, that of recognizing itself in the reorganization of action brought about by the categories of feelings. In thought a new type of structure is created which is no longer direct objectification of energy—as is action—but that of abstraction. The self, which discarded its objectifications in order to know the emotions and recognize in them feelings, pursues in its affective analysis an operation which destroys nothing but extracts what is similar and dissimilar. From these extractions comes the new structure, which is thought. There is no break in the constitution of feelings (which comes from the classification of emotions), and the intellectual classifications (which comes from the classification of objectifications).

Although thought exists all through life, it is a discovery of adolescence because thought then becomes aware of itself. This discovery is a genuinely new awareness that comes via the conscious formation of feelings and the designation of the categories found in the set of emotions. The stuff to be made explicit already is in both affectivity and the objectifications in the form of energy, but the sensitivity to attributes of this energy generates awareness that one is directly associated with an aspect of the self not yet studied. The adolescent undergoes the new experience that one can individually direct one's thought by this awareness and can genuinely assert what is happening within oneself. Therefore assertion is a characteristic behavior during adolescence.

But since the impact of this material on one's consciousness results from recuperated energy and the re-examination of previous objectifications, one has both a solid sense of reality and a feeling of the unformed, the labile. From the first a cockish certainty may result, from the se⁄ ond a sense of weakness and uncertainty of the ⌐ntent of one's awareness. This explains why it is n⌐ possible to have a set of responses which are stabl⁄ ᶜ⁴ʳᵤgh to lead us to a standard classification of what auᴐlescents think in most matters. No longer exclusively engaged in action, they see more than what they perceived in actions and situations. Not yet certain of what they perceived actually in a field they have not sufficiently articulated to themselves, what will matter most for them is the field as perceived and objectified by society.

Thought is the perception of a fleeting new sensitivity to what accompanies emotional upheavals: one can assert that some things are happening to oneself which were not happening before. Now since the upheavals are determinedly pursued by the adolescents as being the true stuff of the awareness of this period—they live within these upheavals—there is no possibility for adolescents to account for the upheavals through the logic of action, which through given actions achieves given ends. Because this logic does not apply, a new logic has to be developed. The time this takes varies with individuals and may cover a few years. But when it is formed it is a logic aware of itself, intellectual logic, the logic that permits lengthy verbalized arguments and stained by the genuineness of the contribution from the reality of organized categories covering from all one has gone through. That "reality" is based on: objectifications which involve perceptions and actions; the stabilization of the energy flow between the sifted newly examined objectifications; and the immediate gathering of experienced data made available by the total re-examination of the content of the self and the settlement of the main issues raised during this hyperactive period.

Still, thought is more than intellectual logic for the latter is the form for social intercourse and the first is capable of transcending experience, present and past, and can find uncharted fields in the accumulated stuff that fills the mind. Because it can transcend experience, it is known as free and hence as a spiritual expression of the self. It gives a new life and a unique tint to what seems connected with one's total experience. Thought can become a source of new statements about what goes on in one's intellect as it becomes aware either of some content that so far had been unnoticed or of some relations between awareness or of some dynamics until then taken for granted. This is intellectual creation. The set of such discoveries goes to form the intellectual material bequeathed to one's creation, some of which may remain in the culture of one or more groups.

Because thought participates in spiritual contagion, it can know its freedom only when it knows that the necessity of thought is spiritually true. It does not seem possible for the adolescent to think outside of the intellectual frameworks of the environment, but the spiritual thought function may seize all the truth which these intellectual frameworks contain. The awarenesses that what they contain is true, that the content of language and abstract knowledge as signs of the creativity of the mind are absolutely justified, is one of the events of adolescence and characterizes it as much as does the growth of spiritual awareness through religion. At this point in the individual's intellectual development it is not logic which justifies the intellect and its products, as will later be the case. Now it is the direct knowledge of the spiritual intellect which brings us to the examination of categories and forces us to construct a logic for ourselves: the mechanism of our thought. The latter justifies the former and makes it acceptable.

Insofar as it is distinguished from logic, thought is a spiritual, human function. The adolescent gives us the proof of this every day, by his refusal to think logically, by his lack of appreciation of logical constructions in the rational sciences, and by the use that he makes of contradiction to discover himself spiritually. No spiritual trouble is created in him by the fact that some of his propositions are self-contradictory, and he can be perfectly loyal to two opposed ideas when they are set out for him on the formal plane. This is an everyday experience for all those who live with adolescents.

We shall examine the education of the adolescent in the next chapter, but it is appropriate here to comment briefly on the lessons for education that follow from our discussion of the discovery of thought in adolescence.

Intellectual education should follow the true spiritual life of the adolescent and take into account these psychological sequences we have just examined. In this way, we shall spare our young boys and girls much time and many frustrations. If we want a strong and well-equipped intellect, we must first create the conditions which will allow the growth of the awareness of thought as a spiritual function—an awareness of its freedom, its creative power, its discriminating use of states of spiritual energy and objectifications. Once we do this the proper function of thought in life will be exercised with vigor and it should be added and emphasized without external pressure, thought being a true spontaneous function and, for biological reasons, forming part of human life, of spirituality. Its form will not necessarily be the rediscovery of a past, of an existing system of thought, as Piaget would have it, but rather as it was for a religion: a discovery, in this instance of the intellectual function, at first within the framework of the intellectual environment, but also, following that, containing the ability of going beyond. Realization of thought in this form will place our students in a time relation to the future, in the only permissible attitude: with respect for originality and expecting its occurrence.

Since it is based on the spiritual state which permits the constitution of feelings, thought is, by nature, a new kind of structure of spiritual energy. It is a structure which uses the links existing *between* objectifications—that is to say, uses affectivity itself —in order to construct itself. This allows it to make use of all objectified life and to enclose it, entirely or in part, in the abstract schemes in which it manifests itself rather than through the objectifications themselves. Whence the mobility of thought in comparison with action, from which it is derived. From this also—the abstractness of thought—derives the possibility of creating or annihilating thoughts (which is only partially true of images).

If spiritual energy is only partly statified in our bodies, in our images, in our actions, it is still less statified in thought, which is almost free energy and whose evolution—by which I mean its increase in content and profundity—is precisely a growth in its mobility, even if, at this price, it loses the property of being energy. Thought is that form of spiritual energy which has reached its proper use in losing awareness of its nature. Thought thinks itself and then begins a conscious intellectual life, a rational life—that of the philosophers. Thought thinks itself by a spiritual act which becomes intellectual, and most men are no longer conscious of thought's spirituality because this act takes place during adolescence, the only moment when contact with the self and affectivity is permanent. Among those adults who pursue their evolution and who have forgotten the spirituality out of which thought arose, intellectual life, whatever its level, takes then the place of spiritual life. For them emotional life is considered of an inferior kind and rationalism takes hold of the mind. But rationalism is incapable of reliving the contact with energy and of finding for itself any spiritual power other than that of reason. The whole of life becomes intellectualized. The intellectual absolute descends on all things, and those who find in the success of rational action—in science—a reason for believing in its absolute, transform the world into a system of abstract relations. The society of these people then gives most prestige and value to those among them whose intellect is best developed, and it offers educational programs that except for intellectual and rational parts, neglect the spirit.

This explains much of the present situation in contemporary society. Not only have we not got enough means to prove the spirituality of man in all its manifestations, but by its handling of the education of the adolescent, an intellectually oriented society has established the lie that the spiritual hierarchy stops at intellectual mastery. It closes the future to its youth because the ceiling it proposes is too low for youth's evolution. It cultivates only the intellectual scaffolding, ignoring altogether the spiritual truth, the soul of thought: dynamic affectivity. Fortunately, the adolescent often brings to bear his own experience. On the one hand, intellectualism loses the "simple minded" and, in rejecting them, limits its life to that of the "driest" of children. On the other hand, the claim to rationalize everything leads to contradictions which are fatal to intellectualism. As it omits religion and all the mysteries and deliberately attacks only the "how," it does not realize that thus it exposes itself to a constant danger in allowing the irrational to exist alongside with reason. To say that truth is only rational and to accept to live alongside such a great number of irrationalities is the greatest weakness of rationalism, which the adolescent cannot judge because he himself fills reason with irrationalities and the intellect with spirituality.

I have argued throughout this work that adolescence should be defined as spiritual experience not as a physiological state. We have just examined how thought, far from being alien to affectivity, to feeling, arises out of them. I believe there is yet another perspective which needs to be reversed in order to furnish us with an adequate framework for the psychology of the adolescent. It is the theory concerning the connection between puberty and love.

In chapter 3, we tried to define love within the framework of a psychology of objectification. We saw how ambiguous the term love is in ordinary psychology. We now see the influence of this ambiguity in the problem with which we are at the moment concerned.

If love is the action of the psyche, there must be a relationship of cause and effect between puberty, a physiological phenomenon, and psychic love. We are familiar with the difficulties which are met by those who are not Freud's disciples in the study of infantile sexuality such as he presented it. In addition to the difficulties which have often been mentioned, is there not also a major difficulty arising from the meaning of the word love? The ideas of sexuality and reproduction have been so closely associated that puberty, which makes the latter possible, has been accepted by all as the ability to experience the former. Freud gives a particularly wide meaning to the term sexuality; by this word he understands the expression of the instinct, of the libido, which at a given moment only takes the form usually designated by this word and which is linked with the preservation of the race. Although strongly attacked, his definition has been very widely accepted. It shows clearly the relative meaning of puberty and sexuality, freeing the latter from too rigid a definition. But it does not in the least explain, except in perfectly understandable pathological exceptions, the still mysterious fact that puberty comes unexpectedly on adolescents.

Certain authors have defined adolescence by the onset of puberty, but they have not been followed. The case is still that the sexual hormones are only liberated very late and that, in their being put into circulation in the blood, the principal role is played by the pituitary, a tissue which is half brain and half gland. Puberty is therefore under the control of the brain, and its arrival seems to wait on something. What is it that will decide this tremendous liberation which will alter such a large number of functions and make the child almost adult from the psychic point of view?

If we accept, as seems to me correct, the idea of maturation as being of physiological origin, we could either deny the existence of adolescence (as for example, does C. M. Fleming in her book *Adolescence**) or we must explain maturation in its turn. Why does maturation take this length of time and why is it manifested in the way that it is?

We have seen that adolescence may be defined as a

---

*C. N. Fleming, *Adolescence*. London: Routledge and Kegan Paul, 1949.

particular spiritual experience, and that the physiological does not intervene as the driving power but
rather as the consequence, afterwards. In other
words, it is not because he is pubescent that the
human being is capable of loving, but because he is
now able to love that he becomes pubert.*

When the child, who has created his frameworks of
action, discovers himself as spiritual energy, his power
of loving appears to him for the first time. He
discovers "the other" as a spiritual being and this
discovery will shift the emphasis of his life, so that it
is led under quite new conditions. We have seen how
he re-examines affectively his relationship with all his
objectifications, how he orients himself towards the
creation of his own thought and his faith. From the
somatic point of view, he now takes stock of himself
and gives to each action its place. He already knows
how to utilize his means rationally in all his actions,
but his field of action may be widened. He will realize

------

*A perspective like the one advanced here, which follows the self in
time and gathers the data of living from what actually happens to each
individual, is helped by the contrast with others perspecting. Interest in
physiology arose less than 150 years ago. The knowledge of the
functions of the tissues and organs changed altogether one's vision of
what organs and tissues were for. In a similar way, interest in behaviors
is changing again the vision of functions. Just as Claude Bernard could
say in 1856 "Functions create organs," it is possible to say today:
"Behaviors create functions" and find that the function of some glands
is delayed so that some behaviors will be capable of coping with their
results of their functioning. This perspective is supported by the
anatomic structure of the pituitary in which the lower half is a ductless
gland while the upper half is brain tissue. Adolescent behaviors,
awareness of love in particular, triggers the brain part to trigger the
chemical part to activate other functionings in the soma.

Similarly, childhood's demands on behaviors require that the growth
of the soma be controlled to the point that children can refine action
before they consider the adjunction of what bulk will bring. These
behaviors are the delaying spiritual mechanisms which put the brakes
on physiological functions, themselves spiritual because they belong to
one's soma (spiritual energy objectified).

his maximum possibility, no longer in acting on action, but in bringing to action his maximum potential energy: in growing. While small muscles are necessary to control action, large ones are needed to realize it to the full, and puberty is a period of rapid somatic growth. In the field of action, the adolescent places all the emphasis on power and not on precision and speed. This new power in the actions suggests to the adolescent that he is a physical energy; the adolescent builds on this framework of feelings which will serve as a basis for his moral experiences.

The same physiological mechanism produces somatic and glandular growth at the same time. As a result of this growth, there appears a being ready to live a complete spiritual life, including that of sexual love and reproduction (which, as I have noted, are not essential human forms but express human possibilities). Puberty is the somatic echo of the attainment of energy. Physically: power. Intellectually: power. Psychically: power. Socially: power.

It is not just by chance that Nietzsche and Schopenhauer have had so much success with adolescents, nor that the psychology of Adler has so many disciples among them. An adolescent quickly understands and adopts the idea and the term "inferiority complex." We are roused by this concept because the true idea behind it is that of power, the feeling of which we all experience in our adolescence.

Puberty and nubility are only connected because in ancient civilizations puberty was an obvious indication of power; today puberty and the age for marriage are no longer synonymous. Procreation does not bestow the right to take a wife; economic conditions must also be favorable. Puberty is no longer a sign of social power. It is one of the somatic aspects of a certain moment in life when many things are demanded of man in addition to the discovery of his spirituality. Puberty itself no longer gives the right to complete love; it does, if it is isolated, allow the sex act, which society today confuses with love. But when the adolescent experiences love, he himself does not give pre-eminence to the sex act as adults do. For him, love is spiritual and the sex act animal. He will perpetrate it, if necessary, but he will rarely find his happiness in it. He will study it, dispassionately, will know it as an external act, but he will not regard it as the image of love.*

This separation of love and sexuality may have terrible consequences for a sensitive youth, torn between his beliefs and those of the environment. For him, love is much more beautiful if pure. It is not love if it be not pure. Many adults believed that the disturbances of youth arise because the adolescent (naturally the male only in a male-dominated society) does not exercise his sexual function and ask society to make special provision for it. The anguish, the degradation which so many adolescents experience in

---

*These comments may sound terribly naive and as if written by someone from another planet. There is plenty of evidence gathered from adolescent diaries, from psychologists' reports to justify the statements about the priority of love from young men and women who may have also indulged, when not in love, in all sorts of sexual practices. The coexistence of these apparently contradictory behaviors corresponds to the two concerns of all of us with affectivity and with objectifications. Since adolescence is so short compared with the whole of life, the preoccupation with pure love during this period may look insignificant as compared with sex symbols and sexual objects. I still maintain that when we understand the workings of affectivity and the true meaning of adolescence, we can realistically reverse the temporal proportion and obtain a ratio of great significance for education. It is not clock time that should occupy us but rather the difference in the intensity of experiencing and in adolescence we discover about love what will be our wealth for the rest of our life.

their contact with prostitutes are the source of much graver conflicts than the presumed ones of abstinence. In order to prove to himself that he is normal, in following the usual practices, he may (to his conscious knowledge or not) permanently degrade himself. He assumes an attitude in which love is but a sexual game and in which, in disparaging the woman, he debases himself. He loses his most precious conquest, his spirituality, and is thrown back on objectifications as such.

The ignorance of our society in matters of love does not arise, as it did for our ancestors, from an ignorance of physiology but in that it identifies love with an act which is not spontaneous and real except when it expresses power, that is to say, when we have become mature because of the growth of all our affectivity by true love.

The sexual art of loving which excites the curiosity of the adolescent leaves him profoundly skeptical. Fortunately, when he discovers love, he recognizes it immediately and desperately wants to preserve it from being sullied.

In all climates the songs of love are similar, and the student who sings parodies would never do so before a woman who moves him. For the adolescent, love is spiritual and love is pure because he has transcended the physiological in his adolescent experience.

6. The Education of the Adolescent

THE education of the adolescent is more difficult than that of any other age. In the preceding chapter we touched on some aspects of the psychology of the adolescent; in this we are going to study various questions.

We must not forget that education is a function of the adult society preparing the young generation for its task of tomorrow. Education, such as adults understand it today, is not only effected by the school, but also results from the multiple action which the environment exercises on the child and from the conditions in which he grows up. We examined in the preceding chapter how we develop our awareness of our growth. Here, we shall consider the deliberate actions of the environment called education. For this we have at our disposal spiritual contagion and inspiration and, according to the level of awareness achieved by adults, they will or will not realize the conscious aim which they propose for themselves.

Therefore, three possibilities exist. The adolescent

may be led either toward an established end, for reasons acknowledged or not, or left without direction in a chaotic and decaying environment, or lastly, be placed upon the true path to his future.

When the state elects, for partisan reasons, to lead consciousness in certain directions, or when religious schools, whose real aim is generally denominational and militant, attract minds by their specific symbolisms, adolescents can only breathe a spirituality previously determined and sometimes do not even know that others exist. That is the first possibility.

The second seems to be materializing today in many environments, when the adults, losing all their own spiritual resources, are no longer capable of inspiring the young, and indeed their spiritual contagion becomes negative. We should recognize that this has been the case in many countries for some years and that we are now confronted with such a confused situation that it is no longer known who is responsible for the existent spiritual disorder nor what to do to get out of the *impasse*. This chaos is in the minds, and the confusion creates a discouraging state of affairs.

It seems, however, that all imaginable means are at our disposal for correcting this situation—yet without there being much possibility of using them. The modern means of reaching the general public, which could so greatly facilitate education, are in fact its enemies: the film, radio, television seem to encourage passivity and serve the propaganda advocated by those who control them; the press propagates a literature and a language often lacking in beauty, as well as slogans which are misleading if not direct lies. Trade unions, social and political organizations encourage frustrations, throw egoisms into opposition and bargaining into the fore. An entirely egocentric social perspective, materialistic and self-centered, is arising and calls itself progressive.

However, each one of these means could be beneficial and lead more quickly to a more rational education which would prepare the new generations more adequately for their future.

It is the third possibility mentioned above, the only really functional one, which merits our attention, and not only from a theoretical point of view. In fact, the future is the time when the lives of today's adolescents will be creative, and it is for this future that we must prepare them. That has never yet been done, apart from a few pioneering schools, that is to say, only sporadically and without continuity.

To prepare for the future has at first no meaning, since "tomorrow is not yet created," and the ordinary man knows only the present and the past, and by a slight extrapolation, the immediate future—tomorrow. Yet, upon closer examination, we can see that this future has no meaning if we consider it only in terms of clock time and mechanical actions (although even for them periodic motion assures a certain perennity). Human life is spiritual life, and the law of brotherhood—that the Elder Brother can inspire the younger—gives a new meaning to relative time. There is no single spiritual time, whatever meaning is given to these words; there is rather a time for each individual. The recognition of spiritual time, which is the stream of consciousness or movement of affectivity or the idea that we are energy, is what is seized in a single act by the adolescent and, according to different civilizations, may lead to all kinds of objectifications. The essential thing is that, as soon as we are aware of time, we know that it is *our* time and that, according to our own rhythm, we are able to raise ourselves up the ladder which the law of brotherhood extends to us—or that we may extend. It is in making this spiritual ascent that relative time becomes manifest. The past experience (in clock time) of the Elder Brother who inspires us, is, for us, today and tomorrow, and will continue to be tomorrow until we have transcended his level. There will stop being a tomorrow, in the sense we have just used it, when the ladder is completely left behind and those who leave it can see nothing beyond it.

Now, this is inconceivable for most men who live within spirituality. Those who live outside spirituality, or think they do, live without hope, are incapable of being inspired and of inspiring. It is true that they would offer no obstacles to spirituality if they were completely empty and nonresistant. But in general, they oppose it through a belief in skepticism and an attitude of resistance entailed in their philosophy, called by them common-sense. So it is today. These people are not capable of measuring in themselves the role of spirituality which, however, is active in them in the form of their belief, materialistic or otherwise. But while denying for themselves the power of spirituality, they nonetheless accord to themselves the power of influence, of determining the views of youth, and they use the power of spiritual contagion to lead the young, directing them towards a static tomorrow, which is the yesterday of the adults grown permanent. Thus, in practice, their denial of spiritual-ity is voided by their recourse to spiritual contagion. But the adolescent who believes in his Elder Brothers and takes their experience as if it were the truth, has born in him a very great uneasiness arising from the opposition of his hope and their skepticism. The environment, which ought to inspire him in order to lead him towards all the tomorrows of conscious adult experience, offers him the spectacle of a spirituality which exhausts itself and creates substitutes for itself. Such, for example, is the race to secure pleasure and material goods in the world of today.

Seeing our youth, one could really think that there was no hope for the future. Carefree and having a security which we did not know, thanks in Europe to the social security laws or welfare state and in America to the general condition of affluence, it is provided with everything, and on account of this, its vision of the world remains immature. The cry "education for responsibility" would not be required if it were not a symptom of the present irresponsibility. How can the "will to give" of the parents—this possibility to grant the children everything, which was copied from the middle class, and has only become possible for the first time quite recently, and only in certain countries—be reconciled with the pressing needs of education for the future? In short, how can one resolve this conflict for adolescents between the uncomfortable reality and the ideal which is full of promise?

The solution that I would offer follows from the position that has been consistently advocated in this discussion (and in my other works), that of considering man a spiritual being. We must adopt affective methods of education, we must illuminate his spirituality. It is his awareness which must be educated, and we must help adolescents to discover themselves in their contact with energy as free, creative beings, capable of going beyond themselves. It is precisely this going beyond which will give each one the certainty that he is master of himself and capable of taking his place alongside his brothers.

The pedagogy of this going beyond stipulates three conditions. It demands:

1. a framework,
2. a knowledge of self, and
3. consistent objectifications.

The framework is a spiritual and dynamic universe. Today nothing less than the entire universe will do for the adolescent—that is his environment; I mean this last word literally: knowledge of self is knowledge of affectivity which objectifies and is aware of itself as energy; the objectifications are those of the creative minds who penetrate further into the universe and there recognize their brothers. We will develop each of these points.

Make no mistakes, the modern adolescent lives at a rhythm, a speed, which we did not know at his age. This world in which he finds himself compels our attention because it is strange to us, but, for him, it is normal, apprehended at once, by a single thought, by all the modern means which have reduced our planet to a minute object. His world does not surprise him. Through the media or travel he can encompass it all, and there is no effort to be made, no heroism in doing so. It is an act which everyone may accomplish. It is not even necessary to be well-to-do to travel; governments take care of that for a large number of people through the Armed Forces.

From the point of view of action and perception, we are quickly out of fashion in relation to the young. For example, they have developed an auditory memory which we (people of my age) do not have, and which our ancestors no doubt started losing when printing replaced it by visual memory.

But we cannot fail to be of tomorrow for the young in the regions where their experience demands growth of awareness and effort. For if we have studied ourselves, we know we have undergone this experience. From the intellectual, social and spiritual points of view, we are of the indefinite tomorrow, above all if we continue to go beyond ourselves and are ourselves aware of what we must attain and transform in order that the universe be totally spiritualized.

If we understand that the adolescent's field must be the whole universe, and if we understand how he must be helped to penetrate it further, we see that his education must no longer be limited to his own country, to national experience. Today, it is an anachronism to consume the irreplaceable years of adolescence in living solely in a national culture. An anachronism which is not only ridiculous, but which traumatizes the men of tomorrow in an often irretrievable way. The adolescent must live his real environment, the universe, intensely. As an adolescent he can do it; later this will be more difficult. He must travel, free himself from objectifications which are neither human, nor absolute, because they are not universal; it is necessary for him both to discard the habits which were meaningful in the more narrow confines of the family, province or state, but which are straitjackets in the actual world of today, and to create universal practices for himself which will slowly become the human culture, the culture of tomorrow.

His field will be the universe, his school social life everywhere—which spontaneously emerges as a variety of human experience in different cosmic conditions. While formerly one traveled in order to learn the customs of others, out of curiosity, keeping them at arms's length, or, since the eighteenth century, traveled in order to appreciate nature (and we still meet it everywhere in the way the Romantics taught us), today travel begins to have a new aim: to experience the social life of the countries visited. Formerly, nature absorbed us: like a mother she presented experiences in which we actively participated, and which gave birth to a love which, from the islands to the inaccessible mountains, from the deserts to the virgin forests, have matured generations of men. Mother-nature is still there, but now that she has given her all, there remains nothing more to discover. Man himself slowly emerges. Not as a curiosity, but as a creative force, as a being who has tackled and perhaps solved essential problems.

More and more direct human contact appears as the only solution to the mutual understanding of men. The education of the adolescent must be itinerant.

After a dozen years passed at home, the adolescent must begin to travel not to "round off his education" as an old adage has it, but to give a shaded, relativistic, sympathetic reality to the mass of elements which the radio, the film, the press, and television discharge on his consciousness the whole day long. As soon as he discovers "the other," he must be shown him such as he is on earth, according to cosmic conditions. The inhabitants of the earth, his brothers, his companions in the adventure of tomorrow, must show him the human solutions brought by their civilization or culture to their problems. A real, cultural relativism alone can serve as a basis for understanding. If friendship and universal love is added to it, then the future is saved.

The education of the adolescent within the confines

of a national or nationalistic school, even with the intellectual windows opening on to other cultures, appears today as a crime against the future. In a sense this proposal is utopian. In another sense—apart from the argument that new types of international schools ought to arise—it is not. Such schools have existed. From 1947-1957, the "Ecole Normale Internationale" conducted experimental international centers with adolescents from many countries. These centers provide a first model for the schools of tomorrow.*

But it does not suffice to send the adolescent out into the universe in order that he recognize himself as universal spiritual energy. This has happened some-times, but too rarely for us to be able to formulate a technique from it. The adolescent, who is naturally in contact with his affectivity and who is spontaneously creating his sentiments, must be led beyond himself to an "affective-intellectual" recognition of himself as spiritual energy. There exist hardly any techniques at the moment for achieving this. The _explosive method_ which we used in the experimental centers, and which I have used since, is sometimes helpful, though far more research will be necessary before refined techniques are available.

The object of this method is to bring the student to a direct recognition of his affectivity. Here, _by way of example_, is an experiment which is somewhat diffi-cult to describe because the words will convey only the intellectual aspect and the reader will not be so vividly aware of the affective element. Those who participated in the experiment are however unani-mous in declaring that, as regards the recognition of

---

*I have discussed the experience of the Ecole Normale Internationale in an as yet unpublished work, _Handbook of Supernational Education._

the dynamic affectivity within them, it far exceeds anything they had consciously experienced previously.

Nobody had been warned of what was going to happen. Three adults and about fifteen adolescent boys and girls between the ages of sixteen and twenty from France, Belgium, England and Denmark were invited to join in a game which, they were told, would help them to understand themselves better. Each was asked to write on a piece of paper the names of the people who were most dear to him. No one looked at the other's lists, which could be as long as desired. The participants were asked to conceive of the people on his or her list as taking a car ride, and they were to suppose that no one knew how to drive save the one making the list.

The lists were composed without reticence, even gaily. Then the remainder of the game was described. En route, a weak bridge is crossed where the car is obliged to stop; it is impossible to go forward or to go back with the car and impossible to get out of it. There remains only one solution: to lighten the load of the car by throwing one person overboard. Whom shall it be?

The harmless game is transformed into an affective tragedy. Immediately, everyone is extremely unhappy and forgets that it is a game. There is nothing to be done, no solution. To throw oneself would be of no avail, since the other occupants of the car cannot drive. The confusion of these adolescents was such that their intelligence was completely incapacitated. When they were questioned on what was stopping them from making a decision, it was clear that on the one hand it was the idea of committing a murder, and on the other, the lack of hierarchy in the sentiments which they attached to the people on their lists. Even when it was proved to them that it was not a question of murder and that it was more serious not to decide on the death of one of the passengers and to cause all the occupants of the car to perish, no choice was possible. One of the young people said that what paralyzed him was having to make the choice himself, and that, probably, he would wait to see if one of the occupants would offer to sacrifice himself.

The experiment was very painful affectively and some of the participants thought it very cruel to propose it; others had a bad fit of crying and sobbing (a response indicating that it would be wise to take certain precautions if the game were to be repeated).

In spite of what the readers may think of the experiment, it contains elements the knowledge of which has escaped us to this day. Remember that the participants consituted a group of mixed ages, nationality and sex. All the participants had the same reaction, a human reaction, proving that the intellect can only deal in concepts and that in the presence of affectivity it loses the alleged control which we willingly admit it has, and that when affectivity is not presented with complete reality where action may intervene, introspection appears to be superficial and the affective dynamics hardly conscious. Nobody could disengage himself from the situation, the participation was so strong that no one remembered that it was only a hypothesis, and it remained useless to remind them of it. At one go the contact with affectivity was greatly enlarged and one's awareness of it much more acute. If such an experiment were again undertaken in solitude by the adolescent, he would be much nearer to his dynamic self after having become aware of all those things paralyzing his action and intellect.

On another occasion, a chance interjection by one English boy—my lord!—led me to propose that he tell us something about the soul. He was a boy who intended to become a surgeon, and his attitude was skeptical and materialistic. His reply was that the soul and spirit did not exist, and that man was merely matter. When I appealed to other members of the group for their opinions, their replies were conventional and academic. Suddenly an idea came to me. I sprang into the middle of our circle, seized the English boy and said: "Come here, you liar!" He changed color, silence fell on the group, and everyone stared at me, thoroughly puzzled. Without speaking I sent him back to his seat, drew a delicate-looking girl forward and gazed at her with a hypnotic stare until she felt dizzy, then sent her also back to her place. I then threw a chair to the ground, selected another girl who was wearing a long dress and told her to jump over the chair. She did so, and returned to her seat. I then sat down and asked the group to try to analyze what had occurred.

Answers were not immediately forthcoming as the effects of the shock were still being felt. I helped the group to recover and we then discussed the three different behaviors. They analyzed the bewilderment and indignation of the boy as moral reaction, the response of the first girl as abandonment of the will, and that of the second girl as a courageous action. The young people had seen for themselves that more than mere matter was in question, and from that point their contributions became increasingly interesting and fruitful, the discussion continuing for two hours.

We shall not examine other experiments conducted

in various ways in order to lead the adolescent to the understanding that he is spiritual energy in evolution. All of the experiments are related to what I have called the explosive method, which, every day, increases our knowledge of the psychology of affectivity in general and that of the adolescent in particular. Since in the process of placing the adolescent before his spirituality one is concerned with acts of becoming aware, it is necessary to create the conditions for these acts, and if the inspirer, the educator, is aware of his role, he can suddenly bring about the unfolding of his students' being toward higher levels. This shock technique can be used at all levels, but a caution is necessary: the technique is difficult to use and necessitates both a relative mastery of situations and much love and humility.

The third necessary condition for the pedagogy of adolescence is what I have called the need for consistent objectifications. By that, I mean that the education of the adolescent demands that the adult spiritual environment provide the inspiration that will help him to achieve an adequate mastery of objective spiritual manifestations which are intellectual and social. The adolescent needs, and the environment should produce, inspirers, educators whose intellect, sense of service, and social mastery are such that he may be filled with enthusiasm for literary creation, science, philosophy, technical and political affairs, social organization. True service requires that the educator draw out authentic creation and not only such mediocre scholastic endowments that, for example, prepare people to pass examinations. Creative sap circulates in too small quantities in our schools, and many adolescents are made to feel themselves empty and uncreative. They are productive, however, and we ought to let them know it, make them experience it, while being careful not to admire too much their spontaneous productions for the very reason of this spontaneity. On the contrary, one would do better to recognize that the child and the adolescent possess all the aptitudes spontaneously, but also remember always, applying the rule first to ourselves, that only the best of our production is worthy of our genius. Creativity was given to us with our spirituality and we should therefore cultivate an aspiration towards the best, the highest.*

Thought has infinite possibilities, which generations of adults have explored for centuries. Adolescents have a right to thought because it is part of their spiritual universe. Social life, which has become conscious only recently, finds its key in the rationalization of human relations, through politics—which is the life of social beliefs, and by everyday 'sociology'—which is organized life without conscious ideal and the field where outmoded politics are petrified. The adolescent also has a right to the assistance of the social life about him to further his maturity and increase his conscious participation in total adult life.

But because he will not participate in adult life all at once, his mastery of it must not be presented to him as a practical or intellectual exercise. Adult life must appear transcendental to him, fill him with a sense of the ideal, of the immanent; it must appear poetic because it is transcendental. Love exists in the adolescent. It is the sense of service which must be cultivated in him and not that of responsibility.

---

*One model for the adolescent is a "Temple of Greatness" where he lives ceaselessly in contact with his Elder Brothers whom he loves and who love him, whom he admires and who inspire him in creating the spiritual atmosphere which sustains him and carries him forward.

Service is the true basis of harmonious social relations in a group, large or small. When an adolescent's awareness is stirred by spiritual contagion and inspiration to a conscious and analytical social vision, it will be impregnated with the sense of service and will support a man useful to his brothers, a man whose counsel will be enlightened by the generosity of love.

Too often in social intercourse one sees the relationship of exploiter and exploited. Too often one thinks that this impasse can be avoided by educating adolescents to become leaders. Love and service do not mean resignation and acceptance of the status quo, when that is to be social stagnation. On the contrary, our adolescents—for whom experience is at the scale of their environment, the universe; to whom human knowledge is the knowledge of all objectifications brought into being by cosmic conditions; whose models are the greatest, most generous, devoted, and courageous; whose affectivity is known as creative energy; whose enthusiasm is assured—our adolescents will at first be timid, but then, with all their strength and sense of service, will be adults, creating new conditions for their conscious life in a human civilization.

Theoretically possible, this education of the adolescent and his spirituality becomes practically possible for all those who dare to undertake it, first because its foundation is psychologically true, and then because the times are auspicious.

For the first time in history, the adolescent is gaining an importance in society, because he is at the stage when man becomes aware of energy and freely chooses from his environment what he wants in order to become spiritually, intellectually, socially mature.

The adolescent counts today because it is around him that gravitates the formation of the human society of tomorrow, completely conscious of its unique spirituality, that of energy.

To educate is to make people aware. We shall educate the adolescent when we make him aware of his original creativity. He will do the rest.

7. Adolescence, the Study of Environment and the Teacher

HERE we shall outline an overview for the whole domain of education, and in doing so we shall review many of the elements in our earlier discussion from the viewpoint of studying the environment—not simply in its physical aspects (though these currently are of obvious importance) but as the totality of the field within which men act. For today's adolescent, this field is the universe.

As we have seen, there is a tendency to reduce the environment to that which is "objectively" accessible. Now if we identify the scientific field with the objective, we notice that modern science studies, for example, animal and human behavior, the influence of the psyche on the soma, etc. Thus, as an "objective" field of study, individual psychological experience can be considered part of the environment. But any limitation seems arbitrary, and in order not to impose limits on an evolutionary science, we shall call environment, the class of all the experience of the individuals who co-exist.

This definition obviously implies that, for us, the

real universe is the universe of perceptions, represen-
tations, actions, sensations, etc. We cannot isolate the
environment to be known from the mind which
knows it, nor that which is known from reality. That
is to say, the only reality which we would accept is a
reality seen through man, objectified by him, a reality
humanized. There is no science other than the
examination of this reality.

The study of the environment affords a review of
human experience undergone by ourselves or transmitted from other minds (by the intermediary of
symbolic or other human processes). The environment comprises by definition experiences concrete or
otherwise, accessible or otherwise, experiences of
geniuses or primitive experiences, but experiences
which have been undergone, or are being undergone,
or will be undergone by some human being.

To know these experiences is to recreate them in
our own mind, our own substance. It is by the
presence in us of a substitute for this or that
experience, that we can say that we have known it,
experienced it in our turn. In knowledge there is a
double movement: an experience and a becoming
aware of that experience. The latter is not always
asserted verbally. Now, the fact of experiencing and
of becoming aware presupposes the existence of a
consciousness which is going to "become" something.
This term, consciousness, is essential when considering knowledge.

If the environment comprises all human experience,
it therefore comprises also the acts of becoming
aware and the states of awareness themselves. Therefore, the most fundamental knowledge of the environment is: *knowledge of consciousness as the*

fundamental element of reality and the recognition that there are other consciousnesses with the same function and the same legitimacy in the constitution of reality.

Now, in the evolution of a mind in the environment, the becoming aware of one's consciousness occurs late while the becoming aware of experience is immediate, for it is not necessary for the awareness to _consider_ its existence when it is assured of this existence by feelings and through action. But when action is essentially completed in exploring the dynamic environment—when action becomes study—the simultaneous knowledge of a knower in ourselves and in others imposes on us the need to search for the knowing. Our awareness of consciousness has at least three forms: thought, scientific empiricism, religious mysticism and love. The projection of these three forms of awareness furnishes three categories of reality: the fields of speculative and mathematical sciences, of natural sciences, and of art, philosophy, and religions.

Historically, the awareness of consciousness initially was revealed in various and manifold forms, and was sometimes considered a useless hypothesis. But today, when science is active in unifying the data of our awareness and has understood that awareness is a phenomenon not only worthy of study but privileged among all phenomena because of its omnipresence, today we are searching for something to oppose to the fragmentation of awareness in the infinite variety of their objectifications (fields of study) and we find that the essential acquisition is that of the agent unifying knowledge, _consciousness_.

There is a hierarchy in knowledge and at the summit is consciousness.

*   *   *

There is no doubt that the aim of education is the maximum growth of each individual, that is to say that education proposes to place each one in a position of experiencing the most advanced elements in the environment, such as we have defined it, in order that he may extend the boundaries of human experience still further. The educational method par excellence is therefore *inspiration*—which operates at all levels, at all stages: the inspiration of genius on its nearest contemporaries, of them on those of the younger generation, then by organizations, symbolisms, rites, and rules, on the youngest. But inspiration presupposes someone to inspire—this is the crucial point which distinguishes our pedagogy from traditional instruction—it presupposes a self, an active and creative awareness, a will active in order to create, creative because active.

Today, because we can look at the whole of evolution at once and can distinguish therein the people who are really our virtual contemporaries, we see experience as humanity moving through a succession of explorations of awareness.

At first embedded in its own somatic structure, awareness slowly detaches itself from this structure to form *images,* a compromise between the awareness enclosed in the structure and the one gained from the extensions through the organs of sense and action. There are two kinds of images. The first consists of the remnants of energy that the soma receives through the senses, these images are capable of being evoked and are recognized as standing for the source of the impact. All images of the people and of the world around are of this kind. The second type of image consists of the energy which the self pours into the organs of sense during sleep or in daydreaming so as to objectify a thought or a project. Soon both types merge together and form one mass of images that the self can act upon to change and make adequate to the perception of the world as it is refined by the awareness achieved by the self.

This mass of images is therefore a substitute for natural and social reality. As the awareness detaches itself from the first objectifications and, in order to facilitate action, builds for itself a universe which conforms to that of others, it recognizes itself as if linked to its first objectifications and at the same time as separated from them.

The existence of the self as existing in itself—which follows from self-awareness—at the same time brings about the recognition of the legitimacy of the existence of others doing so by the act of love which is so exclusive.

In fact, in love, there is this paradox, that although we may only know ourselves and our reality may be the only reality, the loved one is completely absorbed in us, is ourself, lives in us, on us. A separate being is integrated. Thoughts, feelings, actions are projected beyond ourselves by someone else who lives in us as intimately as we ourselves.

Adolescence as we have seen, is the period in our lives when this double awareness of ourselves and of others is effected. It is the period when the moral formation, the consciousness of the good, the just, the great, the beautiful, the eternal—in a word the consciousness of love and of awareness—takes root, going beyond us and beyond itself.

Thus at this point in the evolution of an individual's awareness, the study of the environment becomes not an intellectual knowledge of the analytic elements which compose reality, but the penetration by a conscious self of a universe which it humanizes at every level of study, up to the moment where, becoming aware of love as a major human function, the social part of the self emerges revitalized, inspired anew and capable of finding its only durable and reasonable basis.

At no level is the self separated from its environment. It cannot be. When the environment is considered as outside it, the separation is an artificial one, though it may very well exist. But such a situation is unthinkable for a self which has preserved in itself its discovery of spiritual time and of love as the foundation for human relationships. It is necessary that educators should understand this fundamental point: to consider the environment as absolutely separated from the self is to create a traumatic situation, and to perpetuate a mistake which common experience contradicts; it is to lose all chances of making education the medium to bring the future into the present.

Human environment must be bathed in humanity. It is by means of its spiritual tools that the human being reaches humanity. It is by perfecting these tools through experience and reflection that reality is constituted by the former and apprehended by the latter. The environment, for this reason, is one with experience, and we return thus to the definition with which we began. The study of the environment, therefore, comprises *the maximum extension of awareness* and is not only a systematic inventory of the variety of human experience, of living things, and of natural and social forms.

How then can this study of the environment be

undertaken? What special place does this study have in the education of the adolescent?

Systematic analysis should be avoided so long as the essential aim has not been achieved: the becoming aware of the self, the will, experiencially, awareness which only becomes explicit towards adolescence. From the nursery school to the university, experience of the environment must be a dialogue, first between the self and activity, then between the self and feelings—the period of adolescence—then between the self and the relational and rational universe, the universe of organized human relations (based on understanding and love), finally between the self and the transcendental universe, conquered by the living generation of poets, scholars, artists, philosophers, and prophets.

This program is still very vague, but it includes the germ of the affective pedagogy of tomorrow, which, by profound experience, extends the particular experience of the child, from his objectification of sensorial and active images proper to sensory-motor action to the liberation of all his energies and the inclusion in himself of all mankind, the only aim proper to our universalist and relativistic era.

Instead of the sterile collecting of photos and newspaper cuttings, instead of classifying, cataloging, exhibiting, etc., as is done today as early as the primary school (and even sometimes in kindergarten), the child will develop by means of a series of opportunities determined by the educator in which the child's awareness, following the laws proper to his stage of development, will be led to the mastery of his objectifications. The child will not operate analytically like the scholar, but rather by the analysis which implies the mobilization of all the spiritual tools in action at a given moment. Permanent, synthetic-analysis—such is the new method of apprehending a selected environment so as to be accessible to the tools at hand and to educate the awareness rather than "furnish" memory.

The role of the entire personality in the act of learning has not been sufficiently emphasized, or if it has been emphasized, it has not been stated emphatically enough that affectivity is always present at all levels in each one of our experiences and that it betokens the presence of the self rather than just the presence of interest, which is an external manifestation of the self. It is not affectivity that occupies the child and it is not from affectivity that one begins at the start of a child's formal education in order to make him acquire knowledge, contrary to what we have been told too often. But it is the affectivity motivating the child that must be educated. Affectivity in itself must receive our attention in order that it may be harmoniously developed in experiences and objectifications of the self that remain in the self and represent the environment.

If we are mistaken in conditioning the fairly young child in his intellectual education by means of classifying, cataloguing and collecting, as it seems so clearly to me that we are, it is none the less true that contact with the rational world ultimately is achieved only by means of science (classifying, cataloguing, collecting, etc.) which is the natural, historic, and human objectification of the rational world.

But adolescents have a profound and pressing task to perform before exploring science. This is to make contact with the world of feelings, to become aware of it in order to be able to transcend it and to enter into what will be tomorrow, since it is there that they will live the conscious, controlled life, the adult life to come.

The environment to present to the adolescent is, as we already have seen by implication, of three kinds: that of love, that of human relations, and that of greatness. In the first the experience of which is so vivid in the adolescent that it leads to physiological maturity, he will recognize a kind of human relation which is beneficial, a source of light and of heroic actions. Love precedes and goes beyond sexuality. In the adolescent, love is identified with the recognition of himself as energy, but as in our society this fact has not yet been recognized and as we have no means of detecting and educating love, its hour often passes unnoticed. At that moment the adolescent finds himself isolated in an antagonistic social environment, materialistic and preoccupied with its own problems. The result is a permanent revolt on the part of the adolescent who knows rebellion to be reality by reason of his authentic experience and by his healthy critical vision of the adult environment.

In our civilization, the church alone until recently has offered adolescents the necessary environment of love. It has thus drained nearly all true love resources except those of delayed adolescents, some of whom have been claimed by political organizations. But it is clear that when the educators of the middle school-age group know adolescents and are freer in their work, it will be to the school that will fall the task of including the educative factors of adolescent love, the spiritual force and the acknowledgement of human identity in all mankind.

But at the same time as there exists love in the adolescent, there is also a variety of human senti-ments proceeding from the simultaneous existence of absolutes which result from different growths. The experience of the variety of affective human relations in fact leads to love, for it establishes the legitimacy of various attitudes—in a word, _through the apprenticeship to relativity_. But there again, in order that we may prepare for tomorrow it is necessary that the adolescent should recognize not only his surroundings, but the diversity of behaviors on the planet— which brings us again to the itinerant school.

In order that education shall be rational and functional and effectively prepare the child for tomorrow, it must take this step forward: to put the world within reach of those who must live in it, in order that they can understand and integrate it. The universe conquered by the last generation of adults must be brought, not by chance, but by education, to the adolescent, who is already furnished with active tools and the power of communication, in order that he may proceed to his proper environment: the whole world. The study of the environment is then that of all the variety of human behavior in communal life, the integration of all these behaviors, and above all their recognition as natural and normal. The study of the environment becomes the effective means for growth of awareness of the human and experimental content of our planet. The youth of today has the right to this knowledge, and it is education's responsibility to provide the techniques by which _this worldwide human environment is rendered directly accessible_.

But the question of presenting the environment to the adolescent is not yet exhausted. For to prepare oneself by love and the direct knowledge of different behaviors, only creates an awareness beyond humanity. What in the environment is there to respond to this new awareness of the adolescent? There is another dimension which it is indispensable to explore, the depth of which becomes educable at adolescence thanks to the unique character of this age. Being capable of loving, the adolescent is capable of giving to others what he feels awakening; being open to influence by others, he is ready to make contact with other lives, in particular to receive what is given through them, either directly or by means of social symbolisms (including religious practices).

The great man, by common consent, is the one who, during his life, has given most to his community, whatever be the importance of that community, and whose life seems to be a miracle in comparison with the contribution of the adolescent, which is negligible. A gallery of great men, then—a "Temple of Greatness"—is for the educator the means to provide the third aspect of the environment which is indispensable to the adolescent. By admiration, the ladder up which our youth will climb, the springboard which will lend its wings equipped to conquer the morrow, the educator will make the effective experimentation of "greatness" really possible.

And in order to do that, intelligence quotients are very secondary! It is sufficient that the affectivity be accessible to the self and that the educator be in a position to experience in himself, for himself, that which propels humanity.

This leads us to the last essential condition for the acquisition of fundamental knowledge, knowledge of the creative self in all its truth and diversity: the role of the teacher.

From my perspective, education has two poles: the integration of experience developed by humanity—

that is to say, the integration of the evolution of humanity (which integration is instigated by the adults and may be realized by transmission from master to disciple or by directly experiencing it)—and the education of the child. It behoves the educator to promote his further evolution all his life, if he is a true educator and not merely an instructor.

To say that the true educator is abreast of general evolution means that the understanding of his position as inspirer of youth compels him to resist being towed along by any of the absolutes of the past surviving to this day in the form of party politics, nationalisms, racialisms, and all other sectarianisms. He knows by his political, religious, social and national experience that intolerance and narrow-mindedness always follow the acceptance of any belief as an aboslute. He knows also by his experience that the absolutes are destroyed in a succession of transcendental acts which are deliberate acts of the self, but which entail a needless expenditure of spiritual energy. What educator today does not know the ridicule that would follow the proposal of a purely sensory material for the education of a normal adult? But how many educators today sense how ludicrous it is to propose purely social techniques for the education of adolescents? Has not a purely intellectual education been given to adolescents for over three centuries?

It is evident that most people today are intensely active socially by means of societies and parties. And under the influence of mass methods of education (radio, films, press, books, etc.) it is also evident that for fifteen or twenty years many educational reforms in many countries have tended to introduce social experience alongside that of the intellectual.

But it has been forgotten that a reform of this sort is essentially the direct consequence of ideas elaborated two centuries ago (by Rousseau in particular) and that the object of the social experiment of the last two hundred years of conscious adult life was to realize the eighteenth-century intuition. As long as other factors were considered responsible for the advancement of men, education was relegated to a minor position. But the situation is different now, and everyone who thinks, thinks of education. The result is a complete reversal of roles.

At the moment, it is to the educator that is delegated the task which formerly fell to the priest, the state, the doctor, and many others. It is for him to look after and maintain the health of children; to fashion the civic spirit and the spirit of devotion to the highest values. To a greater and greater extent, the priest, in every religion, sees himself as an educator, or delegates his function to the educator; the doctor goes to the school to examine and receives enlightened information from the teacher; the state expects from the educator the technological orientation which will increase output and therefore the state's revenue, civic education which will make of each child a citizen adapted to the necessity of governmental rule, enthusiastic for social and military functions, etc.

Briefly, it is recognized that the social framework rests with the educators and an attempt is being made to make them primarily into social workers. However, the social framework is an abstraction since it is essentially fluid and within it live the adults capable of initiative and capable of changing things. The educator must realize that there is a contradiction in submitting to a social educational order, in the sense in which it is ordinarily understood. Since society is dynamic, the function of the educator in order to serve the social cause is to prepare youth for the tasks of tomorrow.

It can be seen from this remark that education for the future is only possible if the educator has transcended the social as well as the intellectual and sensory-motor elements in his environment.

In this sense, to transcend the social element involves a double operation.

1. It means that one must have explored it thoroughly and experienced for a time its fundamental, constituent elements;
2. It means that one must have penetrated a new universe which includes the social elements as one of its essentials as well as other elements, but which revitalizes these elements through a new growth of awareness of the universe.

It is not therefore a question of transcending without experiencing and neither is it exclusively concerned with the social element.

The new universe which is open to the educator of today—educator of tomorrow in so far as he is a complete adult (and this is a sine qua non condition)—is the universe, implicitly conquered by the spiritual vanguard of our time, which I have called *relativistic*.

It is the universe of the co-existence of variety— temporal variety and human variety, each the consequence of the other. Of all men, the educator in particular must contain within him all ages of humanity. By his capacity to love he carries in him all possible human behavior capable of expression. He recognizes all behaviors as equally comprehensible. He does not judge them by absolute standards, but in relation to each other, all being considered together.

Once this is understood, he bases his educative techniques on bringing them all to light in order that the human invariants, if they exist, may appear and the diversity justified. His universe being the whole universe and at the same time the human universe—a humanized one—he has no respite until his pupils, his disciples, his fellow students have conquered: the whole of the universe open to science and all the science at hand in the universe to be conquered; and all the variety of human experience and through that, wisdom, defined as the collective experience, whose progress is continuous. The educator will transform Human Experience into human experience and expand the latter until the former be apprehended in order to be assimilated.

To the educators of today falls the task of reliving, rethinking the whole of education, in order to put it on a level with contemporary awareness, and to formulate the universal and relativistic techniques which will put the entire environment at the disposal of the rising generation. But these techniques will only be found and transmitted when the educator is liberated by the transcendence of all the past and has entered fully into the universe of the future.

This task, although gigantic, is not beyond our means. From the most humble educator who, each year, is in contact with seven or eight pupils in a hidden village, to the director who presides over the destinies of national and international educational organizations, the task is the same: to have the courage to recognize our position as guides, as inspirers of the generations of tomorrow, in contrast with the politicians who guide the adult generation of today, and the static groups, such as the traditional societies and churches, which drag the past into our midst. Being relativistic, we accord them their right of place, but at the same time, we claim a place alongside their static absolutes, in the name of evolution, demanding the liberty to make way for the birth of tomorrow in the hearts of each one of those who are socially entrusted to us.

In essence our action is revolutionary; it is the only revolutionary action since tomorrow is never the same, and we have the duty of living it for the others so that humanity may completely relive the individual experience of our true Masters, of whom we become the disciples as soon as we have integrated their pioneer experience.

This radical transformation of the educator conforms to the radical transformation of the idea of environment and of the new hierarchy of knowledge.

Appendix A.
On Modes
of Thought*

THE nature of thought processes (thinking as an activity) is still very little understood. People think, and as a result new ideas, new visions, new theories become available. But almost no one knows whence these come and how they develop.

Now, the ordinary man has on the whole little occasion for original thinking. He is, however, able to produce mental structures and mental behaviors which permit him to reach satisfactory conclusions, and this convinces him that his thinking is operative. This kind of process can be called thinking to a pattern because it utilizes the conventional stereotypes most people are accustomed to. In such a way a man may solve a business problem successfully, through recourse to the intellectual processes and environmental factors within his everyday experience. Thus we can say that in addition to the kind of original thinking which permits the unknown to be

---

*This essay, in a slightly different form, originally appeared in *Main Currents in Modern Thought,* vol. 17, no. 4, March-April, 1961.

grasped or the familiar to be blown up so that it yields new aspects, there are *modes* of thought that form the background of conventional thinking.

The distinctive modes of thought can be roughly described as being isomorphic with language. It is well known that languages are limited: no one language can express all varieties of thought and feeling. For this reason translators often miss meanings, since they start with the presumed content of statements rather than with the intimate experience which the writer tries to convey in words; some writers cannot be rendered properly in certain languages. Thus it is that languages act both as vehicles and as filters for thought.

Because of this, it might seem that if men could learn one common language they would understand each other more completely. But it is not possible to say that their understanding would be even slightly greater than it is now, for it is the spirit of languages that betrays thought not the basic vocabulary. Nonetheless, anyone who lives a language and gains its spirit acquires a mode of thought at the same time. It is the writer's experience that there are as many modes of thought as there are languages, and that the modes approach more closely to each other when the languages that objectify some of their aspects are also close. This fact may result in a clarification of the different modes of thought along the lines of work already done by philologists.

Scientific thinking seems to have adopted mathematics as its language. But we cannot speak of either scientific thought or mathematics as being this one thing or that one thing. It is only when we talk superficially that we can define the scientific method in a single clear statement. To my mind, each endeavor of scientists to enter more deeply into the mystery of the universe has required a renewal of the spirit of science. In fact, I would go so far as to say that there is no more *a* scientific method than *an* artistic method or *a* mystic method. Descartes's method, for example, turns out to be just analytic thinking which needs amendment when confronted with challenges met outside classical mathematics.

Scientists use all sorts of devices in their work in order to gather more light upon their problems and find a fruitful track to follow through the maze of probabilities. Empiricism, analogy, models borrowed from other fields of experience—all these things and many more play a role in whatever progress the scientist is capable of making in his search. If we read Kepler or Faraday, we become convinced that the conquest of the unknown is not to be won through a mere sifting of evidence or study of the literature of the subject: it requires a renewal of the self. Trial and error, participation, are of the essence of any search.

When we speak of the scientific method, we usually mean an attitude of mind that contains both skepticism and the capacity to remain undiverted if one's ideas are found to be inadequate to meet the challenges being examined—though these two qualities are but rarely displayed by scientists. The scientific method is indeed a mode of thought which is open: always ready to adapt itself to the reality encountered, never rejecting anything that is not in conformity with predetermined schemes, and constantly trying to develop the means that permit real understanding of the unknown.

This process, in mathematics, requires emotional neutrality and a conscious commitment to the dynamics implicit in the study—that is, the inferences which appear through equivalences and algebraic transformations. The edifice of existing mathematics is the formalized body of definitions, theorems, and proofs which constitutes the so-called language of science. But mathematics is also a creative activity displaying diverse modes of thought. It is this fact—the presence of creativity in mathematics—that creates gulfs between the generations, for one person is not even able to figure out what another conceives to be obvious and immediate. Therefore, if we try to oversimplify our concept of mathematics and define it as one specific and limited thing, we are as much in error as when we try to limit science to one kind of experience.

In forgetting the human, unpredictable element in scientific endeavors, we lend ourselves to the mixing of issues and create those stereotypes and pseudo-problems that admit of endless discussions and no conclusions whatsoever. For instance, it is generally assumed that engineering is a product of science, and that successful technology results from a developed science. As a matter of fact, however, engineering is a mode of thought which has been developed by Anglo-Saxon empiricists, and it is far from being the only scientific frame of reference. Insofar as the rapid growth of the physical sciences required apparatus of an ever-increasing complexity, the development of these sciences was closely related to the development of engineering: in the West, technology thus advanced side by side with physical science. Nevertheless, not all efforts at understanding the universe of experience fall within the engineering mode of thought. The Greeks had a science for which they did not use mechanical models; the Indians have always been primarily interested in meeting outer truth through inner truth; the ancient Chinese looked for a universal key to men's behaviors in the various aspects of their reality. These different approaches all achieved remarkable success in extending man's understanding of reality.

If science represents modern man's efforts to know what is, and to reduce his own interference with what is, then man's various ways of getting at truth must all be taken into account. If we give priority to the engineering mode of scientific study, and deny validity to other modes, we operate from a bias that will only hinder us from meeting what cannot scientifically be ignored.

The test of the value of any scientific theory is generally considered to be its capacity to predict. This would be an acceptable standard if the predictive power of concepts were not arbitrarily limited to what is of value to scientists. Because Western scientists are mainly interested in technological progress, they tend to ignore what is going on in other areas—yet they still feel entitled to call themselves scientists. It is one thing, however, to be humble in one's approach to the mysteries that surround us, and quite a different thing to shut one's eyes deliberately and deny that the mysteries are really there. No present biological theory can account for the reversal of physiological functions used in Hatha Yoga (evidence of which has been gathered quite scientifically), yet biologists do not hesitate to discard such data and still affirm that their models are complete and capable of prediction. Although no present theory accounts for the presence and the unique characteristics of living organisms and processes on this earth of ours, scientists move confidently about on it, pronouncing negative judgments upon concepts which disagree with their own, inadequate though their concepts are to the facts. Again, there is no present theory which even begins to encompass all that we know of man through history and experience. No one knows, for example, exactly what the meaning of childhood is. Yet educators act as though they comprehend it completely. And psychologists proceed on the assumption that they understand a human being—even though they disagree among themselves, and adhere to different psychological schools from which they exclude each other's views.

The bias that has here been labeled the engineering mode of thought was at first mainly evident in the United States, but it is quickly taking possession of all minds in the West and is moving outside that natural area of growth. Practical results in applied science are claimed to be a justification of attitudes in science itself. Knowledge that cannot be embodied in devices is called primitive; areas of experience that escape translation into blueprints and instruments are thought of either as being liable to such translation one day—or as being unrealistic.

But fortunately not all thinkers are following this track. The man who realizes the limitations of any mode of thought and is alert to the insidious interferences of one's own preferred mode upon the set of experiences being studied, cannot but feel that another way of dealing with the matter might be more adequate and fruitful.

Two examples suggest that many modern dilemmas might be resolved if we could make ourselves more sensitive to other modes of thought and develop them explicitly, both individually and in groups.

The examination of education reveals that there are

many components at work within it: social, personal, technical, epistemological, and so on. The trend is now to concentrate on one of these aspects, or even on a small facet thereof. By so doing, we are far from considering the problem of education as a whole, and in fact we cannot expect to find answers to any challenges except those of which we are already fully aware. But what of those educational challenges which are as yet unformulated?

To approach the issue from a different starting point, we have not sufficiently studied the history of knowledge from the point of view of how to meet total situations in their complexity. Still, it is clear from what has been achieved thus far that *true breakthroughs in any direction have been the result of syntheses rather than analyses.* By flooding a complex situation with light from every direction we illuminate areas which a single beam of light could never reach. Too little effort, however, is put into learning how to think in a complex way about complex things; too much effort is still devoted to splitting problems into minute factors that have little relation to the original, total challenge. Squadrons of research workers, applying the engineering mode of thought to improve modern laboratory techniques, can accomplish a great deal. But these methods have not been successful in meeting the challenge of education, except in those areas wherein engineering solutions are valid (such as conditioned reflex instruction and memorization). To work constructively on the problems that confront education as a whole, the mode of thought which I have termed *complex thinking* must be explicitly cultivated.

In order to understand children, we may need another mode of thought which I have elsewhere referred to as _multivalent thinking_. This term describes the process needed to meet the intellectual activity of children, who use, as a matter of course and for quite some years, the _suspended judgment approach:_ they cannot be convinced until they find permanencies in the world around them.

Multivalent thinking is a mode in which the mental structures which are being formed maintain their dynamic links, so that the individual can normally bring in alternatives in the process of growth and of experience. In multivalent thinking, the classes of elements which form the content of thought are indeterminate in number and always operative via a new attribute. In order to learn to talk, children spontaneously adopt this kind of attitude, because words correspond to concepts whose extensions form classes and children meet them as such in the ambiguous environment. This is done naturally and without anxiety, and is rarely followed by a breakdown of the learning process (which would take place if children labeled objects rigidly).

As we know, children in all cultures learn to speak the language of the environment, and sometimes more than one language, quite easily. My own experiments in teaching foreign languages and mathematics in various parts of the world have confirmed the fact that present concepts of education result in changing the natural multivalent mode of thought in children into rigid univalent cultural modes which exclude many possibilities of human thought and make them appear strange, curious, even unnatural. Because adults adhere to their own mode to the exclusion of any other, communication between people breaks down. Children are naturally free from such adherence to a mode of thought in which they are not as yet rigidly fixed, except insofar as it is formalized in the language they use. So the mode of thought of children may be the opening that will permit men to understand each other far better than through the medium of a common language which is artificially created or adapted from one of the highly elaborate languages that already exist. Success in maintaining a multivalent mode of thought in people as they become adult may also lead to a solution to the other problem mentioned above: the need for more people who can think in a complex way about complex things. In our highly perturbed societies, yet to become one humanity, this need is very acute.

We now know that thus far in our history we have barely lifted a corner of the veil of ignorance, barely opened a few windows upon the vast expanse of deeper experience. If we want to push forward the frontiers of our understanding and make full use of all the attempts mankind has made to understand its challenges, we must question our own mode of thought and see clearly what it includes as well as what it leaves out. Perhaps then we shall move more boldly in education, and give it the ability to look ahead while at the same time enabling it to make use of what is true in our children's means of grasping a fluid environment.

Modes of thought form an area for research that would bring together anthropologists, psychologists, epistemologists, linguists and educators. In such an enterprise, each participant should be fully aware that our enlightenment depends upon his work, but also that far more light will be shed if more than one mode is alive and operative in him and in each of his co-workers.

Appendix B.
Notes on World Consciousness, the Environment and Human Education

I*
The past discovered its "universals" slowly. At first there was religious faith. This faith in a Church became *the* Faith; *this* Church, *the* Religion. And it was believed and affirmed that to educate man was to educate the follower of this Church, to the exclusion of all others. And still today, in certain circles, this same assertion is heard.

Then the universality of reason was discovered. And it was thought that the education of the intellect was the only universalist education. The analytic intelligence had to be educated—exclusively. The rest would follow automatically. Western civilization attributed a superiority to itself to which its definition alone gave it a right. Those peoples who had not developed their intellect in similar ways were enslaved and exploited on the pretext that they were sub-human.

Reason, thus, in fact, ceased to be universal, and

---

*These remarks are drawn from an article that appeared in *Culture Humaine*, Paris, 1948.

this recognition set a new problem which Rousseau and the Romantics attacked: the equality of man in the state of nature. Civilization became the offender. To educate was the universal function of nature, which made man by its laws and human groups by social contracts. Societies were the various manifestations of these natural laws in action, and the economy of each group established the natural level which these laws could cause man to reach.

The new "universal" was a social one. Man was no longer a rational animal, but a social animal. To educate was to demonstrate the social character of every human action and to prepare children not for the simple use of rational thought, but to play their part in a group.

Various interpretations of the social order were historically discovered, each one crystalizing in a political party which proceeded to identify itself with the "universal" social order.

In order to characterize the social groups, a static concept was proposed and it was called culture. There was not one culture, but many cultures, juxtaposed in space and time.

Today, most of the solutions put forward to resolve the conflict arising from the multiplicity of interpretations of the social order, consist in a merging of cultures or in a cross-fertilization of cultures, while at the same time somehow keeping each one separate. The familiar difficulty of suppressing while preserving (described by Hegel) is introduced, and it is supposed that it can be resolved by changing cultures—instead of enlarging awareness.

Here we touch the heart of the problem.

We find that, for the most part, contemporary awareness is centered within the social order, which is a creation of man and a human function. Awareness today is most readily reached through social matters, and it is by social means that solutions to the present difficulties [post-World War II] are being proposed.

Since social education is now favored within the national framework, and since the universality of the social has been accepted, the same educational process as exists in the national framework is proposed on a world scale. Social education within nations and education for world citizenship, it is suggested, can be conducted simultaneously. The latter is envisaged as a simple extension of the former. It is only a question of scale.

In short, if the social order is really universal and if social education is possible in national groups, it follows that the new worldwide education ought to be based on social education and in consequence that awareness of the world should be created by the comparative study of cultures (UNESCO).

But the social factor is now known to be relative, the same as reason. Now that we know the variety of all that men have learned about the existence of others, the social absolute has been replaced by complex human elements, variously mastered, understood and utilized. The new worldwide awareness consists in the recognition of the humanity of all of these elements, whose relative distribution gives rise to the diversity and justifies it.

In particular, it is evident that social education itself is based on affective and rational education. Without love, there can be no lasting and beneficent social relationship; without reason, there can be no understanding of the economic and legal laws which facilitate the material progress of the group.

Worldwide education without *complete* affective

education is meaningless today. It is by educating for universal love, by bringing out all its individual varieties and by the intimate recognition of each individual at the heart of all collective varieties, that worldwide education today appears as the only reasonable, true and possible one.

To believe that human education is possible without educating for the love of one's neighbor in a harmonious common life, simply perpetuates the errors of the past when it was thought that it was possible to bring together different awarenesses by means of words. It is the same sort of mistake as expecting that by putting cultures side by side, their scientific, artistic or technical virtues would cause them to become united.

A new and active method is required: the creation of a true world consciousness for everyone, not only for adults or for some adults.

It is a question of a renewal of social awareness, of rational awareness, or simply of awareness, which today must be based on a real and human affectivity that is developed by the inhabitants of the world for the inhabitants of the world. This is what we have become now, inhabitants of the world, and this is our aim in education for world consciousness, to educate our awareness to comprehend the new state.

Illuminated by this world consciousness, the educations of the past (in turn universalist, active, analytical, social) will become enriched by human affectivity, human education, only possible now and the only kind of education which does not create modern monsters, exclusivists of all denominations, the only kind suitable for the emergence of man in the spatio-temporal universe, shot through with humanity.

World consciousness cannot manifest itself exclusively in the form of world citizenship, which is only
one aspect of it, nor in the form of scientific
rationalism or of religious faith; it must be manifested
in all creations of man, at all levels of human
evolution. It is by embracing all the varieties of
human experience that human awareness, which is in
essence universal and simply human in actualization,
can be possessed.

Only those who have this worldwide awareness are
the educators of the future, the real educators of
today. They will ensure that tomorrow will contain
love, understanding, and the creation of this real
unity of the world and of the science of the world,
which is within our grasp.

II* There are two problems that make the
relationship of the child with his environment difficult. On the one hand, there is the evolution of
society in which the small village communities have
been replaced by the metropolis, the big city; on the
other hand, there is the rapid development of
techniques which radically transformed our mastery
of things and of the world.

As long as man only walked or used beasts of
burden, the distances which he could cover in his
journeys were very limited and he formed an image of
the things around him which readily became static.
Apart from the rhythm of the seasons and some
disasters and accidents, everything remained the same

---

*These remarks are drawn from an article that appeared in *Culture
Humaine*, Paris, 1949.

in the peaceful life of the inhabitants of such small communities. There the child grew up without too many shocks, attracted by a number of stimuli which, although exciting for his developing mind, provided only limited scopes. His games, the fantasies he indulged in, for all practical purposes never went beyond the limits of what nature and the customs of his group furnished him with. A tradition could arise and be sustained in such a community. Naturally, the traditions varied according to the geographic or climatic character of the place, but they all had two characteristics in common: their limitation and their stability. The natural and social environment were entirely at the disposal of the child. The whole was on a scale such that it could be almost totally and instantly absorbed. Different groups gave different meanings and forms to a life that was essentially the same: survival in a certain place by means of the natural facilities or those created by the skill of man. Hence, the formation of this multitude of natural and social environments determined by geography on the one hand, that is to say by the accident of nature, and, on the other hand, by forms which human creativity could take in this natural environment.

But this ability of man to invent and conquer has allowed him, in a few thousand years, to produce the means of traveling by land and sea, which have brought the different groups into contact, either peacefully through commerce, or violently through wars. The merging of one culture with another has produced bigger and more articulate societies, of many and varied cultures which were sometimes united in civilizations. These civilizations broadened the concept of environment by their extensiveness, and, as a result, broadened the relationship of the child with this environment.

As long as these multiple civilizations existed, sometimes even independently, in a more or less unlimited area, there was a sort of cultural absolute which characterized each of them. This absolute, centered as it was on moral values and on the manifestations of nature within the geographic framework of a given civilization believed that they formed a hierarchy, each one always attributing the highest place to itself, and on the other hand, that there was created an attitude of scorn if not of hatred on the part of each civilization for the other civilizations. The child growing up in such an environment acquired the attitude, through education and by life in general, that the section of humanity to which he belonged and the part of the known world that he inhabited were alone divine creations; the rest only deserved to be subjugated and conquered.

Two or three attempts to create universal religions, extending beyond the accidental boundaries where the people who founded these religions happened to be born, suffered the fate that resulted from the excessive compartmentalization of early humanity. The universal religions embraced each other, fought each other, were subdivided and, like political, ethnic or economic communities, did not attain the permanent unity to which they aspired.

The appearance of technology and science in the Western world has facilitated the realization of the universal awareness so much sought after by religions. Science was universal from the start, and Technology was understood by *all* men as soon as they were mature enough to master relatively simple mechanisms. The existence of science and technology created a precedent, an ideal which was never realized by religions: the participation in the well-being of all by all those who could attain direct experimental truth. In its rationalism, science has deep roots in all civilizations. Its neutral character allowed it to penetrate all environments and become the most effective link between men, still separated by frontiers, languages, religions, political and economic regimes.

But in themselves, Technology and Science brought a much more profound change: the speed of scientific development in the last two hundred years, which has enabled a few generations to conquer the earth in all its aspects. The constantly increasing speed of travel, the ever greater range of communication, the greater breadth of economic organizations and economic manifestations such as war, the multiplication of dangers, have forced men, first to an intensity of awareness unknown until now, and secondly to a more comprehensive awareness which brings the reality of the rest of the world into the lives of everyone.

It is in these circumstances—which are completely new to man, who has experienced in two hundred years a greater range of evolution than in dozens of preceding centuries—that we find the most radical change in the relationship man-environment and, more particularly, the child-environment relationship

It is therefore no longer surprising that the modern generation demands a way of life unknown to our fathers and that it finds it quite natural to be plunged into a dynamic world which is breaking down all barriers, whether physical or spiritual. It is not surprising either that, receiving the stimulation from the film or the radio and television—which propel them in an instant from one end of the world to the other, from one artistic style to another, from one political opinion to its opposite—our youth should naturally believe that the world is at their own scale, that their awareness is eminently worldwide, as opposed to regional and national.

But this is not all. Science has conquered the universe for man—the physical universe and nuclear energy—which, in space and time, make the inhabitants of the earth the little masters of this immense unknown. By means of giant telescopes and nuclear laboratories, human consciousness is spreading beyond earth into the universe, just as it once passed from geographic regionalism to the whole world.

Although the environment of modern man is no longer as easy to understand as that of our ancestors, modern consciousness, which has reached the stage of development in which it contemplates all that it has conquered, is in a position vis-a-vis the environment relatively similar to that of our ancestors. The bewilderment one feels in ignorance is banished when the mind is enlightened by science. Then we can regard our universe, the environment of our modern children, with the serenity of the pastor running his eye over his flock. This is the great lesson which education must learn from this evolution: *consciousness is always at the same level as its conquests.* This environment which we now know how to come to grips with and describe in detail, which we are able to pass on in a dynamic way through all the instruments of science and technology, is the real environment which must be incorporated into our systems of education.

The study of the environment is therefore no longer a "survey" of the school's surroundings, a technique that was appropriate for a static civilization. It is rather the development of a vision in an accelerated system, and of an awareness which, beginning with the child's body itself at the start of life, will be projected out to the confines of the universe, embracing all natural and social manifestations in all their temporal and spatial diversity. This is only possible by means of a school system that is *nomadic* as soon as the child transcends his immediate environment. Provision must be made for this nomadic system, which appears to be the only functional one today.

No education which does not lead the child to the apex of the awareness of his time can be functional; today this awareness is of the universal.

Through reason and love man is outstripping all the forms which have been proposed to him and is actively preparing himself for the beginning of a new phase which all the world recognizes as the "universal" civilization. A universalist education corresponds to this civilization and *ipso facto* the environment of the modern child is broadened and expanded, incorporating *all* that technology has discovered and will go on discovering every day.

III*

A human education must provide modern answers to the problems which civilization presents to all of us, and at the same time incorporate the universal life values which have been a tradition in religious teaching. More explicitly, a human education must seek to cultivate the aptitude present in

---

*These remarks are drawn from an article that appeared in *Main Currents in Modern Thought,* vol. 15, no. 4, March 1959.

every individual to live a full life of the spirit within each level of experience. To this end, all levels must be related to the whole man.

Instead of making a concession to the needs of the body through physical culture, in human education the body is recognized as the instrument and the incarnation of the spirit in man. Through knowing and respecting the capacities and limitations of the body, it is possible to extend the range of its experience so that the individual can link it more harmoniously with his own levels of creativity. The object of this kind of *somatic education* is not a competitively heightened type of performance, but rather a more complete knowledge for the individual of his range of mastery over his own body. Enlightened awareness of this kind can lead to increased mobilization of the self through perfection of the arts of breathing, walking, climbing, crawling, jumping, swimming, relaxing, gathering strength, and enduring. Thus physical challenges may be overcome without strain or undue fatigue.

Somatic education aims at knowledge of bodily action, so that in later life this action may have the same effortless quality as the physiological functioning which has been learned spontaneously during the first months or years of life.

Within human education, the training of the intellect is based on opposite premises from those which assume that academic performance must be based upon high I.Q. averages. A universal education cannot afford to allow social or academic prejudices to blur reality. The work of the intellect is an attribute of every functioning mind. Children, at a very early age, use analytic powers to distinguish likes from unlikes; they experience the apprenticeship of a whole language with complex structures and appropriate symbols. The symbolic games and spontaneous drawings which they create at the age of five to seven are of such complex structure that no school work, including mathematics, can ever compare with them. For human education, it is only necessary to think of educating the intellectual powers of each individual through the means of exercises that extend the range of these powers in their normal, spontaneous state. This should be the aim and the method—rather than the reliance upon the set exercises which have figured so largely in formal education until now.

New methods of presenting languages and mathematics can prolong spontaneous intellectual activity. Children are able to take these easily in their stride, demonstrating that only ignorance on the part of teachers has confused the issues with regard to education of the intellect.

Experience in the teaching of languages and mathematics proves that what was attained only by the exceptional child in the past can now be achieved by almost every child. For a good deal of scientific and technological knowledge can be presented in terms of awareness of the self in dialogues with the universe of energy. Thus it is now possible to achieve in five years of study—say from the ages of six to eleven—a range of experience for which it has been assumed that at least twelve years of study are necessary. Because the inspiration is different, because the experimental background deliberately invokes the learning mind, the knowing spirit, rather than a response to formal teaching and syllabi, results are distinct and unique.

By intellectual education, I mean education which

provides the extension of the powers of the intellect confronted by: real and multifarious problems; wide realms of analytic knowledge concerning classifications; logical and empirical reasons; hypothetical thinking about relations (mathematics), sense data (physics), and growing and varying systems (biology, history, sociology).

But if man can think, still more can he feel and sympathize. In human education, direct experience of the dynamics of one's own emotions and of mastery of the self over emotional life is deliberately cultivated.

Since, as the child grows, he is not only accumulating experience but also recognizing the *quality* of experiencing, he becomes capable of living his experience either directly or vicariously. This he could already do symbolically by the extension of his actions, but now the life of others, if presented in terms that are true to his experience, becomes integrated into his own life. A child, a person, grows by contact with others, just as he grows by suffering and by solving the problems presented in relating to others and to himself.

History is a field of predilection for growth. Therefore if we select for our pupils those aspects of history which can become a "temple of greatness" for them to visit and live in, the whole of their spirit may be directed towards what is greatest in mankind through that spiritual contagion which moves in some men so deeply and clearly and can give those it touches the dimensions of devotion (and of self-denial) which all religions say are within the reach of everyone.

Literature, in which art can make man even larger

than life, is able to extend intuition of the reality of others and of depths of experience beyond the limitations of personal existence. Great books have the power of inspiration because they move us deeply; they can change our lives either through what they bring to our notice or what they stir in us.

Education is much more than the acquisition of skills and techniques. No school can pretend to have educated its students if it has not been able to give them some experience of what, in every man, witnesses the work of the spirit. And more, it must be able to make the child aware that he, too, participates in that energy which makes the world identical with him in the intimate sense that both are of one nature.

If human education has more to offer the child than traditional education, it lies in this: it never forgets that every child has the right to a full affective development—the development of his own humanity.

Art is another of the distinctive features of human education.

The unique contribution which art can make to the education of every child is that it keeps him always in touch with the springs of his own creativity. The value of artistic production is slight in comparison with the significance of a realization by the individual that his universe of experience is never complete, never closed. If others have been able to act upon their gifts in order to extend their range of understanding and achievement, and thus extract new meanings from experience, the child can do it also. The child cannot be (and does not want to be) the equal of geniuses who have left their names and work for many generations, but he can meet himself in the dialogue with his own powers, transforming clay into shapes, colors into designs, sounds into melodies, movements and experiences into words and silence into meditation and prayer.

In short, the inspiration of human education can take hold of all subjects, all disciplines and recast them into new formulae.

Geography leads to an awareness of one's habitat which starts by being the mother's womb, and ends by being the cosmos.

History nourishes individual awareness with the experience of others, and provides a perspective which limits the ego and discloses other ways of being.

Science enriches through knowledge of power over things, and gives an intimate relation between the mind and a universe in which man's penetration is extending further and further.

Mathematics is awareness of the dynamics of relationships, and furnishes in all men the means whereby experiences, colored by the senses, are replaced by a model in which only the relationships are preserved. On this model the dynamics of the mind allows new readings, which in turn lead to new awareness of the situation, and so to new action. These may mean, again, new power over things.

Languages are the channels of symbolic communication between man and man, becoming more accurate as the experience is more schematized. They are essential for elimination of the solitude of being.

Art is the field of the dialogues of the self with its own creativity.

Somatic education is a way to knowledge of one's body, which leads to the mastery of functions, and hence to harmonious being.

The list presented here is neither exhaustive nor

merely theoretical. A much more fully detailed treatment of each point would seem necessary in order to allow the internal consistency of the proposals to reveal itself, and thus permit a start upon their implementation by educators.